INTRODUCTION OF THE EURO AND THE MONETARY POLICY OF THE EUROPEAN CENTRAL BANK

INTRODUCTION OF THE EURO AND THE MONETARY POLICY OF THE EUROPEAN CENTRAL BANK

Shigeyuki Hamori

Kobe University, Japan

Naoko Hamori

University of Marketing and Distribution Sciences, Japan

 **World Scientific**

NEW JERSEY · LONDON · SINGAPORE · BEIJING · SHANGHAI · HONG KONG · TAIPEI · CHENNAI

Published by

World Scientific Publishing Co. Pte. Ltd.

5 Toh Tuck Link, Singapore 596224

USA office: 27 Warren Street, Suite 401-402, Hackensack, NJ 07601

UK office: 57 Shelton Street, Covent Garden, London WC2H 9HE

Library of Congress Cataloging-in-Publication Data
Hamori, Shigeyuki, 1959-
   Introduction of the euro and the monetary policy of the European Central B / Shigeyuki Hamori,
Naoko Hamori.
     p. cm.
   Includes bibliographical references and index.
   ISBN-13: 978-981-283-842-1
   ISBN-10: 981-283-842-2
   ISBN-13: 978-981-283-843-8
   ISBN-10: 981-283-843-0
   1. Monetary policy--European Union countries. 2. Euro area. 3. European Central Bank.
I. Hamori, Naoko. II. Title.
   HG930.5.H36 2010
   339.5'3094--dc22

                                                                                      2009040975

British Library Cataloguing-in-Publication Data
A catalogue record for this book is available from the British Library.

Printed in Singapore.

To Makoto and Hitoshi

In January 1999, the efforts of the European Union (EU) to establish an Economic and Monetary Union (EMU) culminated in the introduction of the euro and the creation of a single currency area. Initially, the euro area comprised 11 countries — Austria, Belgium, Finland, France, Germany, Ireland, Italy, Luxembourg, the Netherlands, Portugal, and Spain — with an aggregate population exceeding that of the United States. Since the birth of the euro, the EU has had the second-largest GDP ever recorded for a single currency area after the United States. The European System of Central Banks (ESCB) began overseeing a unified monetary policy under the leadership of the European Central Bank (ECB). To enable this unification, every EMU member state had to relinquish the right to pursue its own monetary policy. The euro was introduced in 1999 with non-cash transactions and, in 2002, it replaced the currencies of the countries that had adopted it. The number of EMU member states increased to 16 with the addition of five more countries, namely, Greece in January 2001, Slovenia in January 2007, Cyprus and Malta in January 2008, and Slovakia in January 2009.

The following can be cited as the reasons for the adoption of the euro:

(1) Establishment of a single market in the EU: The EU's predecessor, the European Economic Community (EEC), was established in 1958 when the nations of Europe wished to create a common market in which people, goods, capital, and services could move as freely as possible. They believed that, by doing so, they could create an economic community that was large and dynamic enough to compete with the economies of the US and Japan. However, to realize such a market, they needed to stabilize the European currencies. The initial idea of currency integration was explicitly advanced in 1970 under the Werner Plan.

(2) Success of the European Monetary System (EMS): In the early 1970s, efforts were made to stabilize the exchange rates of the currencies of the EU member states as the first step toward creating a stable currency area. These efforts, which included the "snake in the tunnel" arrangements of 1972 and the inauguration of the EMS in 1979, reduced exchange rate fluctuations between 1979 and 1985 by 50 percent compared to what they had been between 1975 and 1979. Then, from 1986 to 1989, the exchange rates further reduced by 50 percent. In light of the success of the EMS, the Delors Report of 1989 proposed a clear schedule for the institution of a single currency.

(3) Achievement of sound fundamentals in EU economies: Moving toward the implementation of a single currency, the EU member states recognized the need for their monetary policies to be more closely coordinated and for their economic fundamentals (prices of goods, interest rates, exchange rates, fiscal deficits, and government debt balances) to be improved. By obliging the member states to take these steps as a condition for EMU participation, they hoped to achieve low inflation, sound government finances, and low interest rates in the participating countries. They also promoted reforms to the public pension and tax systems, as well as other structural reforms that individual governments had failed to implement successfully on their own.

At this point, it will be useful to review the characteristics of the ECB's monetary policy. The policy strategy is based on "two pillars" for maintaining price stability. In the May 2003 revision of this two-pillar strategy, the ECB redefined the first pillar as an inflation rate (the growth rate of the Harmonized Index of Consumer Prices [HICP]) that is below but close to two percent over the medium term. This effectively set a lower limit with regard to deflationary risk which was a problem that had been growing on a global scale at the time. Yet, the ECB still stated unequivocally that it was not employing inflation targeting, and that it would not implement a mechanical policy response to actual inflation rates. Indeed, throughout its history, the ECB has never announced specific deadlines for achieving price stability. This is in marked contrast to the Bank of England, the central bank of the UK, which has adopted inflation targeting.

The second pillar of the ECB's monetary policy is the establishment and public announcement of a reference value for the growth rate of the M3 money supply. The ECB has announced this reference value every December since 1998, but the value has remained unchanged at 4.5 percent. This 4.5 percent value is calculated based on the following assumptions: (1) HICP growth of less than two percent in the euro area, (2) economic growth trending in the 2.0–2.5 percent range, and (3) a fall of medium-term M3 velocity to annual rates of 0.5–1.0 percent. However, it eventually became clear that the actual M3 growth rates had exceeded the reference rate (4.5 percent) ever since the ECB began pursuing its own monetary policy. Moreover, the M3 growth rates had been high from 2001 onwards, in light of the growth of the short-term convertible securities holdings of parties outside the euro area. In other words, money was shifting from long-term financial products to more liquid short-term ones amid a global economic slowdown. When the markets became aware that this was happening, their faith in the M3 statistic declined significantly and the ECB was rebuked for its use of the M3 growth rate as a policy target. Yet, remarkably, in spite of the harsh criticism against it, the ECB chose not to abandon the M3 growth rate as a policy target but rather to simply downgrade it from first-pillar status to second-pillar status. By maintaining price stability through the control of inflation and the management of monetary policy, the ECB believes that sustainable employment and income creation can be achieved over the long term. The ECB also avows the high significance of currency supply trends as leading indicators of inflation. While the ECB believes that inflation control is a key concern, it is also convinced that the close monitoring of the M3 money supply is crucial for the overall strategy of preventing factors such as excessive liquidity from creating asset bubbles. On this point, the ECB has diverged from the positions of the Japanese and US central banks, both of which have been deterred from ascribing too much importance to money supply in light of its extreme susceptibility to specific factors and the difficulty of accurately gauging its velocity.

The ECB sets the overnight market interest rate (Euro Overnight Index Average [EONIA]) as a directly controllable operating target. Specifically, the bank tries to steer the EONIA to a desirable level by adjusting three key interest rates. First, it sets two policy interest rates — the marginal lending facility rate and deposit facility rate — to form a ceiling and floor above and below the EONIA. Next, it sets a third key interest rate — the main refinancing operations rate — to steer the EONIA toward a desirable level.

Monetary policy and fiscal policy are the two principal tools for achieving macroeconomic stabilization in the euro area, just as they are in other economies. However, in contrast to the case of other economies, the monetary and fiscal policies of the euro area are managed by different forces. The former is centrally controlled by the ECB, while the latter is controlled individually by the governments of the countries that have adopted the euro. Consequently, the ECB faces serious hurdles in trying to maintain a stable monetary policy whenever the fiscal conditions of the euro area countries take a turn for the worse. To mitigate the difficulty, rules on fiscal discipline have been established for the euro area countries via the Stability and Growth Pact.

The launch of the euro as a single currency worked against the pre-eminence of the US dollar as the currency of record for the global economy. To date, the euro has been well received as a new international currency. Whether the euro can match the status of the US dollar as a global currency clearly depends on the success of the monetary policy of the ECB.

The euro area is a unique and exceptionally important currency area for two reasons. First, it is the largest single currency area ever to be created in an industrialized region. In this sense, the euro area is enormously important as a test case for those contemplating the establishment of new currency areas in East Asia, North America, or other industrialized regions. Second, the euro area was established by sovereign states who, in spite of various divisions and challenges, agreed as peers to peacefully and autonomously create a single currency area. Thus, from the outset, the euro area has differed considerably from the currency areas created by countries that are allied with one another through pre-existing colonial relationships. With respect to regions emerging from developing status and forming currency areas, the euro area can serve as a model case.

Now that the ECB and euro have entered their 10th year, this book attempts to apply recently developed econometric methods to examine the monetary policy of the ECB — the guardian of the euro — from various perspectives. We hope that the analyses in this book will contribute substantively to the understanding of the significance of the euro area and the future of the euro currency.

The content of this book is presented in nine chapters.

The EMU is exceptional as an economic and monetary union that has been realized among major sovereign states that did not have an underlying political union at the time of the inception of the single currency area. In Chapter 1, we outline and discuss the developments that led to the realization of the EMU.

Chapter 2 analyzes the stability of the money demand function with both aggregate and panel data for 11 EU countries, namely, Austria, Belgium, Finland, France, Germany, Ireland, Italy, Luxembourg, Netherlands, Portugal, and Spain. First, we find that the money demand function is stable with respect to M3. This arguably supports the suitability of the focus of the ECB's monetary policy on M3 money supply. Second, we recognize the stability of the money demand function with respect to not only M3, but also M1 and M2. These results suggest that the ECB should consider adopting M1 or M2 growth as a reference value, depending on how conditions change over time.

Chapter 3 empirically analyzes the Taylor-type policy response function of the ECB with monthly data from January 1999 to December 2007. We find that the long-term interest rate plays an important role in the policy reaction function. As Kristen (2003) points out, this suggests that the long-term interest rate may serve as a proxy for the public perception of long-run inflation.

Chapter 4 empirically analyzes the term structure of interest rates with panel data from the euro area. Specifically, we focus on cross-section dependence. Our results show that the expectation hypothesis is compatible with the short-term and long-term interest rate fluctuations in the euro area if we appropriately consider cross-section dependence in the model. The results may also provide evidence of the effective functioning of the fiscal rules in the euro area.

Chapter 5 empirically examines the issue of budget sustainability for the 11 euro area countries that are examined. Our analyses here call into question whether the fiscal performance of the euro area is sustainable over the period between 1991 and 2005. However, in the subsequent period from 1997 to 2005, we demonstrate that the fiscal performance is definitely sustainable. This supports the notion that the rules on fiscal discipline are serving their purpose and that the fiscal deficits of individual countries are steadily decreasing.

Chapter 6 empirically analyzes the relationship between the yield spread and the future output growth rate using both aggregate and panel data from the euro area. Our empirical results clearly show that the US yield spread plays an important role in explaining the future output growth in the 11 countries that are examined.

Chapter 7 analyzes the stability of the investment-saving rates using panel data from the euro area. We find that the relationship between saving and investment tends to be rejected for recent samples. This may indicate that the stable relationship between saving and investment rates tends to disappear as capital markets become more integrated in the euro area.

In Chapter 8, we use the long-run structural VAR (vector auto-regression) approach to analyze the sources of the real and nominal effective exchange rate fluctuations of the euro in comparison with the US dollar and Japanese yen. After identifying two types of macroeconomic shock (real and nominal), we uncover the sources driving the movements in real exchange rates. The evidence presented indicates that real shocks are the dominant explanatory factors behind the real and nominal effective exchange rate fluctuations of all three currencies. We also find that the influence of real shocks on the movements in real and nominal effective exchange rates is somewhat stronger in the euro area and Japan than in the United States.

Chapter 9 examines the background, current status, key issues, and future prospects for euro-area enlargement. Looking at both individual countries and country groups, we discuss the characteristics of each and the issues that they face. Four groups are examined: (1) the EU member states that did not participate in the final stage of the EMU in 1999, when the euro was introduced; (2) new EU member states that became EMU participants; (3) new EU member states that have participated in ERM II to date; and (4) new EU member states that are not participants in ERM II.

The content of this book is partly based on research papers that we have published in *Economic Systems, Applied Economics Letters* and the *Economics Bulletin*. We would like to thank *Elsevier, Taylor & Francis* and the *Economics Bulletin* for granting us permission to use this research, although the content has been substantially revised. The research of the first author was supported in part by a Grant-in-Aid from the Japan Society for the Promotion of Science. The research of the second author was supported in part by a Grant-in-Aid from the Japan Society for the Promotion of Science and the University of Marketing and Distribution Sciences. Last but not least, we would like to thank Bhupathiraju Shalini Raju and Daryl Chan Li Beng of World Scientific Publishing Co. for their excellent editorial work.

Shigeyuki Hamori

Naoko Hamori

About the Authors

Dr. Shigeyuki Hamori is a Professor of Economics at Kobe University in Japan. He received his Ph.D. from Duke University and has published many papers in refereed journals. He is the author of *An Empirical Investigation of Stock Markets: the CCF Approach* (Kluwer Academic Publishers, 2003) and the co-author of *Hidden Markov Models: Applications to Financial Economics* (Springer, 2004) and *Empirical Techniques in Finance* (Springer, 2005).

Dr. Naoko Hamori is Professor of Economics at the University of Marketing and Distribution Sciences in Japan. She received her Ph.D. from Nagoya University and has published many papers in refereed journals.

Contents

xviii   *Introduction of the Euro and the Monetary Policy of the ECB*

History of the EU Monetary Union

1.1. Introduction

Just over a decade has passed since the euro was introduced as the single currency of the 11 states of the European Union (EU) — Austria, Belgium, Finland, France, Germany, Ireland, Italy, Luxembourg, the Netherlands, Portugal, and Spain — unifying the monetary policy under the European Central Bank (ECB) from January 1999. The policy management of the ECB which spans multiple independent states was first viewed with caution, but it has achieved a measure of success in the face of a variety of challenges. As a result, the euro has established its status as an international currency second only to the US dollar. Furthermore, the number of states that participate in the monetary union (officially called the "Economic and Monetary Union", or EMU) has grown to 16 with the new additions of Greece in 2001, Slovenia in 2007, Cyprus and Malta in 2008, and Slovakia in 2009.

This chapter attempts to outline and consider the kinds of developments that led to the bold experiment of realizing the EMU in the EU. Table 1.1 provides a brief history of the EMU.

1.2. Various Experiments Toward Achieving the Monetary Union

1.2.1. *Werner Report*

Since the establishment of its predecessor, the European Economic Community (EEC),[1] in 1958, the EU has sought to realize an

---

[1] The name "EEC" was later changed to the European Community (EC) in 1967, and to the European Union (EU) in 1993.

Table 1.1. A Brief History of the EMU.

Jul 1952	West Germany, France, Italy, the Netherlands, Belgium, and Luxembourg ("the Six") establish the European Coal and Steel Community (ECSC).
Jan 1958	The Treaty of Rome comes into force, establishing the European Economic Community (EEC) and the European Atomic Energy Community (EAEC or Euratom).
Jul 1967	The Treaty of Brussels comes into force, unifying the above three Communities to form the European Community (EC) comprising six countries.
Jul 1968	Establishment of a Customs Union.
Dec 1969	A framework for economic and monetary integration is hammered out by EC Heads of State at the Hague Summit.
Oct 1970	Publication of the Werner Report.
Apr 1972	Establishment of the "currency snake" system.
Jan 1973	The United Kingdom, Ireland, and Denmark join the EC (nine countries).
Mar 1973	Transition to the joint float system.
Mar 1979	Establishment of the European Monetary System (EMS) including the Exchange Rate Mechanism (ERM).
Jan 1981	Greece joins the EC (10 countries).
Jun 1985	Publication of the White Paper on the Completion of the Single Market.
Jan 1986	Spain and Portugal join the EC (12 countries).
Jan 1987	The Single European Act comes into force; revision of the Treaty of Rome.
Apr 1989	Publication of the Delors Plan, proposing a three-stage plan toward the realization of the Economic and Monetary Union (EMU).
Jun 1989	Spain joins the ERM.
Jan 1990	Launch of the first stage of the EMU.
Oct 1990	The United Kingdom joins the ERM.
Dec 1991	Agreement on the Maastricht Treaty regarding the European Union; agenda for the second and third stages of the EMU revealed.
Apr 1992	Portugal joins the ERM.
Sep 1992	The United Kingdom and Italy leave the ERM.
Nov 1993	Establishment of the European Union (EU).
Jan 1994	Beginning of the second stage of the EMU.
Jan 1995	Austria, Sweden, and Finland join the EU (15 countries).
Jan 1995	Austria joins the ERM.

(Continued)

Table 1.1.   (*Continued*)

Dec 1995	The Madrid European Council selects the "euro" as the name of the EU currency unit and finalizes the schedule for its introduction.
Oct 1996	Finland joins the ERM.
Nov 1996	Italy rejoins the ERM.
Jun 1997	Agreement on the Amsterdam Treaty (the New Treaty on the European Union) (established in May 1995); final agreements on the Stability and Growth Pact, the New ERM (ERM II), and the legal framework of the euro.
Mar 1998	Greece joins the ERM.
May 1998	Decision is reached that 11 countries (Germany, France, Italy, the Netherlands, Belgium, Luxembourg, Ireland, Spain, Portugal, Finland, and Austria) will enter the third stage of the EMU.
Jun 1998	Establishment of the European Central Bank (ECB).
Jan 1999	Beginning of the third stage of the EMU; the ECB commences financial operations; introduction of the euro. Launch of ERM II with Denmark and Greece as the initial members.
Jan 2001	Greece joins the EMU (12 countries).
Jan 2002	Circulation of euro banknotes and coins begins.
May 2004	The Czech Republic, Slovakia, Cyprus, Latvia, Estonia, Lithuania, Hungary, Malta, Poland, and Slovenia join the EU (25 countries).
Jun 2004	Slovenia, Estonia, and Lithuania join ERM II.
May 2005	Cyprus, Malta, and Latvia join ERM II.
Nov 2005	Slovakia joins ERM II.
Jan 2007	Slovenia joins the EMU (13 countries); Bulgaria and Romania join the EU (27 countries).
Jan 2008	Malta and Cyprus join the EMU (15 countries).
Jan 2009	Slovakia joins the EMU (16 countries).

intra-regional integration of markets to enable the free movement of people, goods, and services in order to establish an economic zone that can compete with the US and Japan. From the early 1960s onward, there was agreement among the six members of the EEC (Belgium, France, Germany, Italy, Luxembourg, and the Netherlands) that economic union and monetary union should be promoted simultaneously; however, movements toward achieving monetary union were not particularly visible, perhaps owing in part to the fact that the Bretton Woods fixed exchange rate system — an international monetary system centering on the US dollar — was extremely stable at the time. The currency crisis that arose in 1969, however, triggered the publication of the first plan toward the realization of the EMU, the Werner Report in 1970.[2] Based on this report, the European Council of the European Communities adopted a resolution in March 1971 related to the realization of the EMU in stages and implemented it retroactively to January of that same year.

The main points of the Werner Report were as follows:

(1) In the final stage of the EMU, the exchange rate of each state's currency will be completely fixed and the liberalization of capital movements will be realized. Moreover, at that stage, it will be desirable to introduce a single currency.

(2) In the final stage of the EMU, it is essential to establish an EC central bank system and EC economic policy implementing entity.

(3) EMU realization in three stages to 1980 will be sought, and the reduction of exchange rate fluctuation bands and economic policy integration will be promoted in tandem.

(4) In stage one of the EMU, the reduction of exchange rate fluctuation bands will begin from 15 June 1971. This will involve establishing a reference rate versus the US dollar with a scope of US dollar parity of ±0.15 percent, called the EEC level. It also involves allowing EC member state currencies to fluctuate in the range of ±0.6 percent relative to the EEC, which means reducing the EC member state currencies' band of fluctuation relative to the US dollar from 1.5 percent to 1.2 percent. In other words, the EEC's maximum band of fluctuation relative to the US dollar (1.2 percent) would undulate within the band set under the Bretton Woods system (1.5 percent), and thus, would come to be referred to as a "snake in the tunnel".

---

[2] Report to the Council and the Commission on the realization by stages of economic and monetary union in the European Community: Werner Report, special supplement to Bulletin No. 11/1970 of the European Communities. The report was named after Pierre Werner, then prime minister of Luxembourg, who served as the group's chair at the time.

However, in May 1971, massive US dollar selling/Deutsche Mark buying speculation occurred in Germany's Frankfurt foreign exchange market, and the country's central bank, Deutsche Bundesbank, purchased a massive 2 billion US dollars to prop up the US currency, which then closed the market. At an EC emergency finance ministers meeting held in response to this event, the EC failed to hammer out a unified position due to a disagreement between Germany and France. The former called for the introduction of a joint float against the US dollar (a floating exchange rate system), and the latter argued for maintaining a system of fixed rates to the US dollar. Thereafter, Germany and the Netherlands moved toward an independent floating exchange rate system and Belgium toward a dual exchange rate system,[3] resulting in a split among EC members on foreign exchange policy. The experiment that was designed to achieve the EMU collapsed without securing a reduction in the band of fluctuation in exchange rates.

1.2.2. *Snake*

The Bretton Woods system was finalized with the Nixon Shock of August 1971, and the Smithsonian fixed exchange rate system came to be maintained with the Smithsonian agreement that was concluded in December of the same year. Under the Smithsonian system, the fixed exchange rate between the US dollar and gold was lifted, the rates between the US dollar and the currencies of other countries were revised, and the bands of exchange rate fluctuation were widened. Amid this massive change in the international currency system, the European economic and monetary union (commonly referred to as the "snake") was launched in April 1972 as a voluntary cooperation entity of the central banks of the EC states. In June of that year, 11 states[4] participated, including Norway and Sweden, which were not EC member states.

---

[3]A fixed exchange rate system for current account transactions; a floating exchange rate system for capital transactions.
[4]The UK, Denmark, and Ireland joined the EC in January 1973.

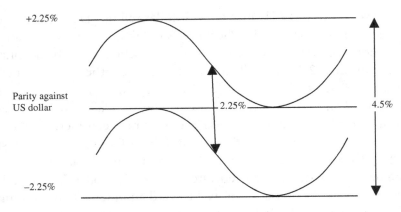

Fig. 1.1.   Snake.

The contents of the snake were as follows:

(1) When the currencies of the states participating in the snake[5] fluctuate ±2.25 percent from the mean exchange rate versus the US dollar based on the Smithsonian agreement, the states must maintain the band of fluctuation through US dollar intervention.

(2) The states participating in the snake are to set a mutual intervention point of 2.25 percent (±1.125 percent), and when that level is reached, their central banks are to intervene using their states' currencies. See Figure 1.1. This system is called a "parity grid."

The name "snake" was designated because the image of the 2.25 percent fluctuation in the currencies of the member states resembled a snake within the 4.5 percent "tunnel" of fluctuation under the Smithsonian system. The snake differed from the EMU in that the member states did not relinquish their currency sovereignty, the snake rejected the possibility of establishing a supra-national central bank, and it phased in a reduction in the band of fluctuation. After the Smithsonian system collapsed in 1973, the snake moved to a joint float (a snake "out of the tunnel") and experienced a change in the number of member states and frequent changes in the parity rate

---

[5]See European Communities Monetary Committee (1974) pp. 58–60, and Hasse (1990, Chapter 3).

of exchange. After the EC currency crisis of 1976, the states that remained in the snake included Germany, Belgium, the Netherlands, Luxembourg, Denmark, and non-EC members Norway and Sweden, and they effectively formed a Deutsche Mark zone, or "mini snake." This mini snake was extremely stable.

1.2.3. *European Monetary System (EMS)*

A.   Process followed through to establishment

During the EC currency crisis of 1976, the UK, Italy, and France, which had adopted floating exchange rate systems fell on hard economic times due to plunging currencies and inflation, while the Netherlands and Belgium which remained in the snake succeeded in quieting foreign exchange speculation through rate hikes and intervention. However, due to the impact of the EC currency crisis and the second oil crisis in 1979, EC states including Germany — the leader among the states participating in the snake — suffered stagflation (simultaneous recession and inflation). Amid economic stagnation, there was growing momentum led by Germany and France in favor of stabilizing the exchange rates within the EC and establishing a stable currency zone. Finally, in March 1979, the European Monetary System (EMS) was established by all EC states; however, its Exchange Rate Mechanism (ERM) was initiated by the eight EC states of Belgium, Denmark, France, Germany, Ireland, Italy, Luxembourg, and the Netherlands, excluding the UK.

B.   Contents

The main contents of the EMS are as follows.[6]

(1) ERM: Similar to the snake and joint float, a parity grid system was adopted. For the strongest and weakest of the EC currencies (two currencies), which reached the upper and lower bounds of

---

[6]See European Communities Monetary Committee (1986) pp. 48–56, and Hasse (1990, Chapter 3).

the fluctuation band of ±2.25 percent, the respective central banks implemented unlimited intervention. However, there were several differences between the snake and joint float. First, instead of median exchange rates relative to the US dollar, median rates relative to the European currency unit (ECU) were adopted. Furthermore, the states that had not participated in the mini snake at the end of the joint float were allowed to choose a broader fluctuation band of ±6 percent, and in addition to the traditional parity grid, a divergence indicator was newly established whereby an intervention obligation was applied to currencies that diverged beyond a certain limit from the median rate relative to the ECU. For currencies that reached this divergence limit, the central banks of the relevant states were called upon to adopt one or more of the following measures: (1) various interventions; (2) domestic monetary policy action; (3) changes to the median rate; and (4) other economic policies. Although these stipulations were non-binding, they were notable in that they marked the first time that available, objective indicators were introduced when EMS member states were implementing economic policy coordination.

(2) ECU creation: The ECU is a currency unit that reflects a basket comprised of certain amounts of each of the EC states' currencies. An exchange rate relative to the ECU is calculated for each state's currency relative to the US dollar. The composition of the ECU basket was set for review every five years; however, it underwent a change each time a new state joined the EC. The roles of the ECU were to serve as (1) the ERM display unit; (2) the basis of divergence indicators; (3) display unit for intervention and credit mechanisms; and (4) the means of settlement and reserve among central banks.

(3) Use of the ECU as a means of settlement: Whereas under the snake, the central banks of the relevant states conducting intervention formed a direct debit-credit relationship, under the EMS, a method for processing through credit and debt column accounts denominated in the ECU within the European Monetary Cooperation Fund (EMCF) was adopted. In addition to the US dollar and the currency of the creditor state, the ECU was also

adopted as a means of settlement. This adoption was made on the basis of the intention to promote a move away from the US dollar in settlements among the central banks within the EC, to foster the ECU as a settlement currency, and to lay the groundwork for a single EC currency in the future. However, in practice, intervention in foreign exchange markets often occurred before divergence limits were reached, and because the selection of an intervention currency was unrestricted, the Deutsche Mark and US dollar were generally used. As such, the ECU saw an increase in private-sector use rather than in public-sector settlement.

(4) Expansion of credit to finance intervention: Intervention funds are essential for ERM management. First, the repayment terms for ultra short-term financial support which emerged as a result of mandatory ERM intervention, were eased. Moreover, short-term financial support — a system to cover temporary deterioration in the balance of payments — saw a nearly threefold increase in both debtor and creditor limits. Medium-term financial support, which is extended to EC member states directly facing imbalances in their balance of payments, saw an approximate 2.5 times expansion in the limits on credit extension.

C. Assessment

The EMS endured for roughly 20 years, until the single currency euro was introduced and the Exchange Rate Mechanism II (ERM II) was established in January 1999 following the EC currency crisis of 1992–93. The following can be cited as the results of the EMS during this period.

First, the exchange rates of the EMS member state currencies showed a stable trend as compared to the currencies of Japan, the US, the UK, and others. In fact, the coefficients of variation among the EMS currencies from 1975 to 1980 were small compared with the Japanese yen, US dollar, and British pound, and the intervals between parity realignment within the EMS became longer beginning in 1980.[7]

---

[7]See European Commission (1980).

However, it is important to bear in mind that the EMS differed as a currency system, using fixed exchange rates which restrict fluctuations, versus the floating exchange rates seen in other countries. For that reason, it is impossible to make a simple comparison.

Second, the EMS achieved certain results in terms of its independence from the US dollar.

Third, monetary policy coordination among the EMS member states moved forward and brought a convergence of economic conditions (e.g., inflation) among those states. This means that the price stabilization policy vigorously promoted by the German Central Bank (Deutsche Bundesbank) which controls the Deutsche Mark — a currency that became the EMS anchor currency — permeated among the EMS member states.

Fourth, the stabilization and expansion of the EMS induced a concrete outlook for the EC's EMU. The stabilization and expansion of the EMS was promoted by the enforcement of capital controls and the advance of economic integration within the EC region. Through the enforcement of capital controls in the second half of the 1980s, massive amounts of foreign capital flowed into the EC. A typical example was the so-called "convergence-induced investment" involving active securities investment in states with high interest rates based on the expectation that the interest rate levels of the EC states would converge to the low interest rate levels in Germany. This effected the stabilization of the EMS without the implementation of parity changes to the currencies of those states with current account deficits, high inflation, and high interest rates. Furthermore, these inflows of foreign capital enhanced the attractiveness of the EMS, promoting the participation of Northern and Southern European nations, including the UK, which had not participated until then, as well as ECU pegging, and contributed to the realization of a stable foreign exchange zone centered around the EMS and spanning Northern and Southern Europe. However, the enforcement of capital controls triggered an unwinding of convergence-induced investment, one of the main factors behind the European currency crisis of 1992–93.

A lesson learned from the EMS experience is that the sustainable nominal convergence of each economy and fiscal discipline of each government are significant in the maintenance of stable foreign exchange rates.

As outlined in the following sections, the EMS member states from the end of the 1980s moved forward toward the realization of the EMU through the introduction of a single currency and establishment of a supra-national central bank. One driver of this was Germany's overwhelming presence in the EMS. Due to Germany's economic strength and the market's strong confidence in the Deutsche Bundesbank, the Deutsche Mark became the anchor currency of the EMS and the intervention of each state's central bank was effectively conducted using divergence from the rates centered around the Deutsche Mark, not the ECU, as a yardstick. As a result, the monetary authorities of each state had to pursue the Deutsche Bundesbank's anti-inflation monetary policies in order to maintain exchange rates against the Deutsche Mark, and often had to implement monetary tightening that ignored domestic economic conditions. Of course, as noted above, this clearly led to the decline and convergence of each state's inflation rate to the levels experienced in Germany; furthermore, it stabilized the EMS and brought confidence in the system. On the other hand, EMS participants France and Italy sought to dissolve the asymmetry with Germany, the anchor currency state of the EMS, and other surrounding states, and free themselves from their dependence on the Deutsche Mark and Deutsche Bundesbank.[8] To an extent, it was because of this that there was a vigorous push toward building the new framework of the EMU.

1.3.   Contents of the Monetary Union

1.3.1.   *Delors Report*

A.   Background

EC states, especially those that were members from the initial launch, shared the perception that it was essential to introduce a single currency

---

[8] See Masera (1988).

for a single market in the EC in order to maximize the merits of that market. There were a series of concrete developments toward the realization of the EMU from the end of the 1980s against the backdrop of advances in economic integration in the form of market integration, the success of the EC currency system, the desire to eliminate the asymmetry between the system's anchor currency state and its surrounding states, and the realization of financial liberalization through such actions as the elimination of capital controls. First, a concrete schedule for realizing the EMU in three stages was proposed in the Delors Report (officially, the "Report on Economic and Monetary Union in the European Community"), which was published in April 1989. This report was compiled under the strong leadership of European Commission President Delors of France, and accepted at the EC summit meeting in June of the same year.

B.   Contents

As evident from the name "Economic and Monetary Union," the EMU is comprised of both an economic union and a monetary union. The Delors Report does not spell out the stages toward achieving economic union. Here, the contents of the monetary union are outlined. Monetary union was to be completed through the following three stages.

Stage one of the EMU began on 1 July 1990. At this stage, the strengthening of fiscal and economic policy coordination among states and the participation of all currencies of the EC member states in the ERM would be realized. Impediments related to private-sector use of the ECU would be eliminated and usage would be promoted.

Stage two of the EMU would establish the European System of Central Banks (ESCB). At this stage, however, monetary policy would be the jurisdiction of each state's central bank. The band of fluctuation in the ERM would be reduced.

In stage three of the EMU, the ECB would implement integrated monetary policy, make decisions regarding intervention with a third country currency and centrally manage official reserves. Moreover, exchange rates would be permanently fixed and a single currency would ultimately be introduced. Moreover, EC common rules and procedures in the area of macroeconomic policy (e.g., fiscal policy) would be accorded binding force.

C. Problems

On one hand, the Delors Report which outlined the three-stage process for the realization of the EMU was epoch-making, but on the other hand, it also left some ambiguity with regard to important matters. For example, detailed stipulations on the transition to a single currency were not established. Moreover, details on the ESCB at the core of the EMU were not discussed and the contents were left ambiguous. However, under the conditions prevailing at the time when there were substantial differences of opinion among various states, this ambiguity had to be a product of compromise to some extent.

1.3.2. *Maastricht Treaty*

A. Developments following the Delors Report

In the transition to stage two of the EMU, there was some opposition to and caution regarding the proposals in the Delors Report to revise and ratify the Treaty of Rome (the basic EC law signed in March 1957 and enacted in January 1958). However, by the end of the 1990s, a series of meetings among governments finally led to an EC summit and an agreement to discuss revisions to the treaty. In March 1990, the European Commission (1990) recommended a method for the issuance of a single currency that would not recognize the currency sovereignty of the EMU member states and the establishment of the ESCB with a high level of independence that would be modeled on the US Federal Reserve System (the US central bank organization). Then, at the Economic and Financial Affairs (ECOFIN) Council held in December, based on a decision reached at the European Council Summit held in June, a schedule was confirmed to compile and complete the ratification of proposals for the revision of the Treaty of Rome by 1992. As planned, stage one of the EMU was initiated in July 1990.

Following these developments, an agreement on revisions made to the Treaty of Rome was reached at the European Council (EU Summit) held in Maastricht, the Netherlands, in December 1991. The Maastricht Treaty (officially the "Treaty on European Union") was signed in February 1992 and took effect in November 1993. This was accompanied by a timetable for moving into stages two and three of the EMU, and it was officially agreed that stage two would begin on 1 January 1994. The Treaty outlined matters other than the EMU, including the establishment and contents of the EU and the strengthening of government cooperation in the political and internal administration areas of the common foreign affairs/security policy and judicial and internal affairs cooperation. Thus, the EU was created in 1993 as the basis of the EC in conjunction with the enforcement of the Maastricht Treaty.

B.   Contents of the Maastricht Treaty

The contents of the Maastricht Treaty are as follows:

Each state was obligated to complete the liberalization of its capital movements and the liberalization of settlement by the beginning of stage two on 1 January 1994, and the European Monetary Institute (EMI) was established as an entity to promote monetary policy cooperation among the central banks of each state. Under the Delors Report, stage two was to call for the establishment of the European Central Bank (ECB). However, as a result of coordinating the opinions of each state, it was decided to first establish the EMI and then to carry out the preparatory work for establishing the ECB and introducing a single currency. With the establishment of the EMI, the EMCF was dissolved. Furthermore, in stage two, the fluctuation band and incorporation rate of the ECU currencies were fixed.

The transition to stage three required the fulfillment of certain economic criteria. If at least eight of the then 15 EU member states met these criteria by the end of 1996, the schedule for the transition to stage three would be determined by a majority vote at the EU summit. If a transition was not determined at that point, only the states that met the criteria would automatically make the transition to stage three from 1 January 1999. The conditions for transition to stage three were as follows: (1) price stability; (2) a sound government fiscal position; (3) low and stable interest rate levels; and (4) stable exchange rates.

After the transition to stage three, the ECB was immediately established as the successor of the EMI, and it began to manage the unified monetary policy. In conjunction with the initiation of stage three, exchange rates were fixed and the ECU was introduced as the single currency.

1.3.3. *EMI Report: The Changeover to the Single Currency*

In order to reduce the costs of the changeover to the single currency and avoid confusion among the public, as well as to sustain an environment that would enable confidence in and acceptance of the single currency euro,[9] the European Commission adopted the "Green Paper on the Practical Arrangements for the Introduction of the Single Currency" in May 1995 and the EMI published a report called "The Changeover to the Single Currency" in November of the same year. In these reports, it was proposed that stage three be divided into three periods from the final year of stage two and the introduction of the single currency.

First, in preparation for the first period, the EMI carried out tasks such as preparing the necessary organizational and legal framework and regulations for the ECB and ESCB to execute business in stage three of the EMU, preparing legislation related to the euro, and developing and testing the euro settlement system (TARGET: Trans-European Automated Real-time Gross Settlement Express Transfer System).

Period one was scheduled to begin in May 1998. First, after determining who would be the EMU member states, there would be action as soon as possible to select an ECB president, deputy president,

---

[9]The name "ECU" was used in the Maastricht Treaty, but was later changed to the single currency name "euro" after the member states strongly protested on the grounds that this was the name of the currency unit used in Medieval France.

and governors, and to establish the ECB and ESCB. In addition, the production of euro banknote and coin currency would commence.

Period two was scheduled to commence on 1 January 1999, marking the beginning of stage three of the EMU. The exchange rates among the euro and the currencies of the EMU member states would be irrevocably fixed and the euro would be introduced in non-cash transactions (book transactions). TARGET also began to function, the euro was used in all operations involving ECB monetary policy and foreign exchange operations, and the issuance of euro-denominated bonds by the public entities of the EMU member states was launched. However, as the euro banknote and coin currency had not yet been introduced, the currency of each state continued to be used for cash transactions. As for non-cash transactions, it was thought that the euro could spread initially from transactions among financial institutions.

Period three was set to begin no later than 1 January 2002. From that date, the euro would officially become legal tender and each state's currency would start to be collected. The complete changeover to the euro would be completed by the end of February 2002 and each state's currency would lose its legal force.[10]

1.3.4. *Amsterdam Treaty*

Based on the November 1995 EMI report at the Madrid European Council in December of that year, the schedule related to the introduction of a single currency was finalized and it was officially agreed that stage three of the EMU would begin on 1 January 1999. At the European Council in Dublin in December 1996, a basic agreement was reached on fiscal discipline rules and new exchange rate mechanisms were introduced to replace the EMS. Then, at the European Council Summit in Amsterdam in June 1997, it was agreed that the Maastricht Treaty would be revised, thereby creating the Amsterdam Treaty (the revised version of the Maastricht Treaty), which was signed in October 1997 and took effect in May 1999.

---

[10]The period for exchanges with the euro by commercial financial institutions was from the end of June to the end of December.

The specific items related to the EMU as prescribed in the Amsterdam Treaty are as follows:

(1) The single currency is to be named the "euro".
(2) The transition to stage three of the EMU is to begin on 1 January 1999, and the single currency in banknote and coin format is to be introduced on 1 January 2002. The details of the schedule are to be implemented in line with the proposals of the EMI report discussed above.
(3) The euro is to become legal tender with legal validity from 1 January 2002. For the period up to then (from 1 January 1999 to 31 December 2001), the euro will be legal tender and exist together with the currency of each state.
(4) The Stability and Growth Pact established fiscal discipline rules for the member states following the transition to stage three of the EMU. The Pact comprised (1) a framework of mutual surveillance for the realization of sound fiscal management, and (2) an agreement on the stipulations and control procedures related to excessive fiscal deficits. Under (1), all EU member states, including non-EMU member states, were required to publish fiscal programs outlining the medium-term fiscal balance targets and the actions to achieve them, and to indicate the fiscal conditions. Furthermore, based on the fiscal programs, the European Commission (the EU executive entity) and the Council of the European Union (the legislative entity) — in this case, the ECOFIN Council — would survey the fiscal management of each state and if it was judged that there was a danger of an excessive deficit in the fiscal balance, the European Commission and the ECOFIN Council would issue an early warning. Under (2), if a fiscal deficit reaches a level exceeding three percent of the nominal GDP, it is stipulated in principle as an excessive fiscal deficit. Sanction procedures were as follows. If the European Commission judged that a state's fiscal deficit would exceed three percent of its nominal GDP, it would draft a report on that state's fiscal condition. Based on this, the Economic and Financial Committee (EFC) would express an opinion within two weeks. Then, referring to this opinion, the European Commission

would report to the ECOFIN Council. The ECOFIN Council, according to a majority decision, would then judge whether the said state has an excessive fiscal deficit and make a recommendation to that state regarding the corrective action that it should take with respect to the fiscal deficit. If even then the state fails to take action, ECOFIN would enforce sanctions. The content of the sanctions was an order for the state to accumulate non-interest-bearing deposits, and if an improvement in the fiscal balance was not seen after two years, those deposits would be collected as a penalty.

(5) Establish stipulations related to ERM II. The purpose of this action was to set a currency stability pact between the single currency euro area and the non-euro area, and to achieve exchange rate stabilization. The contents were as follows: (1) replace the EMS and ERM with ERM II at the beginning of stage three of the EMU; (2) make participation in ERM II voluntary; (3) establish rates centered around the euro, not a parity grid system determining a central rate for all of the currencies participating in ERM II; (4) set ERM II fluctuation bands at ±15 percent, as under the ERM; (5) the ECB and the central banks of the states participating in ERM II are to carry out voluntary and unrestricted intervention at critical levels in this band of fluctuation, with the euro as the currency used on those occasions; (6) the ECB and the central banks of the states participating in the euro area (EMU member states) are able to terminate market intervention if it is judged that the stability of the euro will be undermined.

(6) Establish stipulations related to the legal framework for euro usage. This is to handle the various issues related to changes in the display currency and the issuance of euro banknote and coin currency. Specifically, this consists of (1) stipulations related to such matters as the continuity of money contracts accompanying the introduction of the euro and the transition to the euro and rules for processing fractions derived therefrom; and (2) stipulations concerning relations between the euro and other currencies.

1.4. EMI Roles

1.4.1. *Establishment and Organization*

Marking the beginning of stage two of the EMU, the EMI was established in Frankfurt, Germany on 1 January 1994. The stipulations related to the EMI were set according to the Maastricht Treaty and the EMI Statute, that is, the protocol attached to that treaty.

The EMI had corporate status and was managed by the EMI Council which was composed of the EMI president, vice president, and the heads of the central banks of the EU member states. It was decided that the EMI president must be someone with an extremely high level of specialized experience related to currency and bank issues, and the appointment of this individual would be recommended by the EMI Council and finalized based on the agreement of the EU summit following discussions with the European Parliament and the EU Council. Alexandre Lamfalussy of Belgium who had served as president of the Bank for International Settlements (BIS) was selected as the first EMI president. The vice president was selected from among the EMI Council members, as they had the right to make the appointment themselves.

1.4.2. *Mission*

According to the EMI Statute, the mission of the EMI was, in fact, broad: (1) to strengthen cooperation among the central banks of the EU member states (hereafter "member states"); (2) to strengthen monetary policy coordination among member states in order to realize price stability; (3) to monitor the management of the EMS; (4) to consult on issues impacting the authority of the central banks of the member states and the stability of the financial institutions and financial markets; (5) to assume the mission of the EMCF, which would be dissolved upon the establishment of the EMI; (6) to promote the utilization of the ECU and supervise it in order to realize the smooth operation and development of the ECU bill and check clearing system; (7) to prepare the means and procedures necessary for the ECB to enforce an integrated monetary policy in stage three of the EMU;

(8) to promote harmony in the member states' practices and laws and regulations related to the collection, compilation, and dissemination of statistics in areas where the EMI authority was to be extended in order to prepare for the transition to stage three of the EMU; (9) to prepare the laws and regulations of operation that should be observed by the central banks of the member states within the ESCB; (10) to supervise the technical preparations of banknote and coin currency for the single currency; and (11) to boost the efficiency of international settlement systems. These can be categorized into three missions and considered as follows.

A. Coordination among Member States' Central Banks and Coordination of Policy

The EMI strengthened the cooperative relations among the central banks of member states and promoted coordination between monetary policies in order to facilitate the transition from stage two to stage three of the EMU. It had to complete the following tasks:

(1) Conduct studies and make recommendations related to the inflation targets and interim money supply targets of the member states.
(2) Monitor and report on the progress of the member states in achieving the standards for participation in stage three of the EMU.
(3) Make recommendations to the member states regarding monetary policy coordination.

In order to complete these missions, the EMI drafted Annual Reports and Convergence Reports each year beginning in 1995, publicized the progress of the member states with respect to their fulfillment of the EMU participation criteria, and submitted these reports to the governments of each member state and to the ECOFIN Council. The Convergence Reports touched not only on the progress of each member state in terms of its fulfillment of the EMU participation criteria (related to prices, interest rates, government fiscal position, and exchange rates) but also on revisions to the domestic laws and statutes of the central banks of the member states as per the Treaty on European Union (Maastricht Treaty). As the ultimate authority on coordination among the central banks of the member states and coordination of monetary policy belonged to the governments of each member state, the role of the EMI was limited to that of an advisory entity.

The EMI Convergence Report submitted in 1995 (European Monetary Institute 1995b) stated that less than 50 percent of the states fulfilled the EMU participation criteria. The ECOFIN Council held consultations based on this report, and at the European Council held that same year, it was officially decided that the plan to begin the transition to stage three of the EMU on 1 January 1997 would be abandoned and instead, the transition would commence on 1 January 1999.

B. Technical preparations toward the establishment of the European Central Bank (ECB)

In order to prepare for the transition to stage three of the EMU, the EMI advanced the technical preparations related to the establishment of the ESCB comprising the European Central Bank (ECB) and the national central banks (NCBs) of all EU member states. The system of the NCBs of the member states participating in the euro area was called the "Euro system". The mission of the EMI was to complete these preparations by the end of 1996 at the latest and outline a regulatory, organizational, operational, and technical framework for the ESCB. The ECB was modeled on Deutsche Bundesbank, the central bank of the EMS anchor currency state, Germany, not only in terms of the bank's organization but in virtually all respects including its high level of independence from the government and its monetary policy tools and operational methods.[11] This is because it was judged to be the best method for the ECB and the euro to inherit the domestic and overseas trust that had been obtained by Deutsche Bundesbank and the Deutsche Mark. The EMI's specific preparations included the following.

(1) The creation of an operational framework for monetary policy and related tools and procedures of the ECB: The main monetary policy tool of the ECB became open market operations centered

---

[11] According to the Maastricht Treaty and Protocol on the Statute of the European System of Central Banks and of the European Central Bank.

around repurchase agreements adopted by such major states as Germany and France. General principles and procedures were also enacted for open market operations other than repurchase agreements (e.g., outright transactions and foreign currency swaps), standard facilities, and minimum reserve requirements. Furthermore, following the German model, the money supply was adopted as an interim target in terms of monetary policy operations.[12]

(2) The examination and assessment of the conditions surrounding revisions to the central bank statutes of the EU member states: The ESCB and the ECB were guaranteed independence from the government by Article 108 of the Maastricht Treaty, but it was essential for the central banks of the member states that formed the ESCB to also be legally guaranteed independence from the government. Therefore, each state was obliged to implement necessary structural reforms, including revisions to its respective central bank statutes, by the end of stage two of the EMU. The EMI encouraged each EU member state to implement the necessary structural reforms to ensure its central banks' independence from the government and, in the Convergence Reports, urged the member states to strengthen the independence of their central banks and assessed the conditions surrounding the revisions to the central bank statutes of each state.

(3) Building an efficient settlement system (TARGET): TARGET is a system for linking large-scale fund settlements in real time within the single currency zone by connecting across national borders the real-time gross settlement systems (RTGS) of the states within the region. Establishing a network linking the central banks of each member state through the construction of TARGET was important because most settlements and transfers accompanying commercial transactions were conducted in the form of increases or decreases in the central bank current deposit account balances of banks and other financial institutions. Another advantage of this real-time gross settlement system was that it lowered systemic risks

---

[12] See European Monetary Institute (1997a, 1997b).

because there was one settlement conducted per transaction. The testing of TARGET began in July 1997 and after the transition to stage three of the EMU, TARGET was managed and operated by the ESCB. The RTGS of those states that did not participate in the EMU were also, in principle, able to connect to TARGET.

(4) The financial data and accounting criteria were unified.

(5) The design, size, and other aesthetic matters pertaining to the banknotes and coins of the new currency were finalized as necessary preparations for the introduction of the single currency.

C. Promotion of ECU utilization and monitoring of utilization conditions

The EMI promoted utilization and monitored utilization conditions primarily with respect to the official ECU. This was because after the transition to stage three of the EMU, it was the official ECU that was subject to exchanges at the exchange rate of one-to-one with the single currency euro. The official ECU was the ECU used, for example, in the medium- and long-term finance and financial support of states within the region and other regions implemented by EU institutions such as European investment banks, in EMS management, and in the foreign currency reserves of the states within the region.

However, the EMI also had to monitor the private-sector ECU that had developed in the form of finance and bond issuances in the private-sector financial markets. This is because substantial concern was voiced among private-sector financial institutions, companies, and investors regarding the sustainability of money contracts denominated in existing currencies, including the ECU, after the introduction of the single currency and the change in appearance of the new currency as compared to the existing currencies, requiring the EMI to implement practical agreements on these matters.

1.4.3. *Authority*

As noted above, the EMI does not have the authority to issue orders or enforcements with respect to the EU member states. However, on the condition of a two-thirds agreement of the EMI Council, the EMI does have authority with respect to the following: (1) to express its opinions or recommendations on related measures to be introduced in the member states and the overall guidelines and enforcement of each state's monetary policy and exchange rate policy, and to communicate these opinions or recommendations on paper to the currency authorities of the relevant states; and (2) to submit opinions and recommendations on policies that impact currency conditions inside and outside the EU, particularly the operations of the EMS, to each government and the Council of the European Union. Moreover, upon the unanimous agreement of the EMI Council, the EMI may generally disclose these opinions and recommendations.

1.5.   Decision Process on State Participation in the Monetary Union

1.5.1.   *EMU Participation Criteria*

In order to promote the success of the monetary union — the final stage of the EMU — it was essential to establish the necessary systems for the introduction of a single currency, as discussed in section 1.4, and to fully advance economic convergence among the EMU member states. The Maastricht Treaty stipulated that the following economic convergence criteria would have to be fulfilled for a member state to participate in stage three of the EMU:

(1) Price stability: Consumer price inflation on average during the year up to assessment[13] shall not be more than 1.5 percent above the average of the 3 countries with the lowest inflation rates in the EU.
(2) Long-term interest rate stability: Long-term interest rates on average during the year up to assessment shall not be more than two percent above the average of the three countries with the lowest inflation rates in the EU.

---

[13]More specifically, at the end of 1997.

(3) Government fiscal deficit: The annual fiscal deficit of the general government (central government, regional governments, and social security accounts) shall not be more than three percent of the nominal GDP, or when the fiscal deficit shrinks on a real and continuing basis and reaches near three percent, or when any move above three percent is exceptional and temporary.

(4) Government debt balance: The public debt balance of the general government shall not be more than 60 percent of the nominal GDP, or it must fall at a sufficient rate toward the 60 percent level.

(5) Exchange rate stability: The currency of a state within the EMS has maintained the fluctuation band established by the ERM for the most recent two years and has not undergone devaluation.

However, the EU offered no official explanation for the basis of computing the figures in these participation criteria and the decision process, resulting in a system that lacked rigor. For example, the three percent figure for the fiscal deficit relative to the nominal GDP which became the most problematic of the participation criteria was said to be calculated loosely by assuming five percent nominal economic growth and asking to what percentage the fiscal deficit would need to be held on a single fiscal year basis in order for the government debt balance relative to the nominal GDP to be kept roughly within 60 percent of the average among the EU member states during the 1980s.[14] Hence, when determining which states would participate in the EMU, one can say that this allowed for extremely flexible interpretation and political judgment about the fulfillment of this participation criterion.

1.5.2. *Participation Criteria Fulfillment Conditions*

Whether the EMU participation criteria were fulfilled was judged on the basis of actual figures at the end of 1997, and at the European Council (EU Summit) in the composition of the Heads of State or

---

[14]See The Nikkei (1997).

Government held in May 1998, the final line-up of the EMU member states was determined.

Table 1.2 compares each state's participation criteria fulfillment conditions at the end of 1996 and at the end of 1997 when they became subject to assessment.[15]

(1) In terms of consumer price inflation, most states had already fulfilled the criteria by the end of 1996, and only one state, Greece, had failed to do so at the end of 1997.

(2) In terms of long-term interest rates, as with consumer price inflation, most states had already fulfilled the criteria by the end of 1996 and only one state, Greece, had failed to do so at the end of 1997.

(3) In terms of the fiscal deficit relative to the nominal GDP, three states — Luxembourg, Denmark, and the UK — had fulfilled the criteria by the end of 1996. The latter two of these states had declared that they would not participate in the EMU immediately. The states that had yet to fulfill the participation criteria took severe fiscal deficit reduction measures, raised various taxes, and implemented expenditure cutbacks to the extent of reducing social security expenditure. As a result, 14 states, excluding Greece, had fulfilled the criteria by the end of 1997.

(4) The criteria regarding the balance of the government debt relative to the nominal GDP was arguably the most difficult of the participation criteria to fulfill. Four states — Finland, France, Luxembourg, and the UK — had managed to do so as of the end of 1996, and as of the end of 1997, there was no change in the EMU line-up.

(5) Exchange rates held stable overall after the ERM fluctuation band was widened to ±15 percent in August 1993. As of the end of 1996, five states had failed to fulfill the participation criteria: non-ERM participants the UK, Sweden, and Greece and ERM members for less than two years, Italy and Finland. This situation had not changed at the end of 1997.

---

[15] See European Monetary Institute (1998).

Table 1.2. EMU Participation Criteria and Fulfillment Conditions.

Participation criteria	Consumer price inflation rate		Long-term interest rate		Government fiscal deficit/ nominal GDP		Government debt balance/ nominal GDP		Exchange rate stability	
	1996	1997	1996	1997	1996	1997	1996	1997	1996	1997
Participation criteria	2.6	2.7	9.1	7.8	3.0	3.0	60.0	60.0	○	○
Austria	1.8	1.1	6.3	5.6	4.0	2.5	69.5	66.1	○	○
Belgium	1.8	1.4	6.5	5.7	3.2	2.1	126.9	122.2	○	○
Denmark	2.1	1.9	7.2	6.2	0.7	-0.7	70.6	65.1	○	○
Finland	1.1	1.3	7.1	5.9	3.3	0.9	57.6	55.8	△	○
France	2.1	1.2	6.3	5.5	4.1	3.0	55.7	58.0	○	○
Germany	1.2	1.4	6.2	5.6	3.4	2.7	60.4	61.3	○	○
Greece	7.9	5.2	14.4	9.8	7.5	4.0	111.6	108.7	×	×
Ireland	2.2	1.2	7.3	6.2	0.4	-0.9	72.7	66.3	○	△
Italy	4.0	1.8	9.4	6.7	6.7	2.7	124.0	121.6	○	○
Luxembourg	1.2	1.4	6.3	5.6	-2.5	-1.7	6.6	6.7	○	○
Netherlands	1.4	1.8	6.2	5.5	2.3	1.4	77.2	72.1	○	○
Portugal	2.9	1.8	8.6	6.2	3.2	2.5	65.0	62.0	○	○
Spain	3.6	1.8	8.7	6.3	4.6	2.6	70.1	68.8	○	○
Sweden	0.8	1.9	8.0	6.5	3.5	0.8	76.7	76.6	×	×
UK	2.5	1.8	7.9	7.0	4.8	1.9	54.7	53.4	×	×

Source: Convergence report 1998 (European Monetary Institute).

1.5.3.   *EMU Member State Decision Process*

Of the 15 EU member states at the time, the UK, Denmark, and Sweden were likely to choose to abstain from participating in the EMU and Greece effectively declared that it had abandoned its attempt to fulfill the criteria. This raised the question of how many of the remaining 11 states would be recognized for their participation in the EMU. Although some of the states failed to fulfill the participation criteria related to exchange rates and public debt balances, all 11 were recognized for EMU participation based on the following flexible interpretations.

First, in terms of exchange rates, the ERM participation period of Finland and Italy was less than two years,[16] but the ERM band of fluctuation in their currencies was relatively narrow,[17] as with the other 10 participants (including Denmark), and it was judged that stability had been maintained.

In terms of public debt balances relative to the nominal GDP, six states had levels exceeding the 60 percent benchmark specified in the criteria but less than 80 percent (Germany, Ireland, the Netherlands, Spain, Portugal, Austria), and two had levels of more than 100 percent, sharply exceeding the 60 percent level stipulated in the criteria (Belgium, Italy); however, it was judged that this would not hinder participation in the EMU, even in the latter case, on the grounds that the states' levels had declined steadily toward the 60 percent level each year.

Such flexible judgments in determining EMU participation can be viewed in the context of the somewhat weak economic basis behind the criteria themselves, as discussed above: the fact that the monetary union, even if it was achieved, would be meaningless if it excluded Germany and Italy, two major EU states; and the political consideration that it would be difficult to exclude Belgium and the Netherlands which had been members since the establishment of EEC. Thus, stage

---

[16] In Italy's case, this means the period after the return to the ERM.
[17] According to the EMI convergence report in 1998, the maximum band of fluctuation from the median rate based on a moving average of 10 business days was 3.5 percent (see European Monetary Institute 1998).

three of the EMU began on 1 January 1999 with the participation of 11 states: Austria, Belgium, Finland, France, Germany, Ireland, Italy, Luxembourg, the Netherlands, Portugal, and Spain.

1.6. General Overview

In this final section, an attempt is made to summarize the factors behind the realization of the EMU in the EU.

(1) History of integration: The EU had a history of economic integration dating back to the launch of the European Coal and Steel Community (ECSC) in 1952 and the European Economic Community (EEC) in 1958, setting the stage for easier acceptance of a monetary union (i.e., the EMU) as an extension of economic integration.

(2) Taking a long time: Approximately 30 years were needed, starting with the snake at the beginning of the 1970s to the realization of the EMU in 1999. Certainly, the formation of the monetary union in the EU was delayed by several years from the initial plan because of the massive impact on Europe due to the dramatic changes in the international currency system, international economy, and financial conditions during this period. However, even without that delay, it is clear from the examination in this paper that the realization of the EMU was a process that demanded of the member states a long period of time spanning several changes of national leadership and the resolve to persist through that period.

(3) Small steps: The EU aimed to realize the monetary union first through the snake and then the EMS, starting with realistic systems that each state could easily implement under the conditions of the time, namely, fixed exchange rates that allowed for a certain amount of fluctuation, then gradually upgrading within the scope of feasibility equivalent to the state's conditions. If the introduction of a single currency and the establishment of a supra-national central bank had been put forward right from the beginning, the realization of the EMU would probably have had little hope of success.

(4) Flexibility and tolerance: The realization of the EMU required not only resolve, but also flexibility and tolerance. In the cases of the snake and the EMS, the basic framework of the systems was maintained while tolerating exceptional measures on a case-by-case basis, including the widening of fluctuation bands within the system, the freedom to leave and return to the system, and even the freedom not to participate in the system.

(5) Leadership: Germany and France, major EU states, overcame their differences, consistently maintained their resolve to realize the EMU, and demonstrated leadership during important phases. This was one driving force for overcoming the various issues, crises, and clashes of opinion among member states to finally realize the EMU.

(6) Shared recognition among member states: Member states shared the basic recognition that sustained progress in the economic convergence of each state, observance of fiscal discipline in each state, and a high level of independence for each state's central bank were important in the realization of the EMU.

Empirical Analysis of the Money Demand Function in the Euro Area

2.1. Introduction

When the euro, a single currency for 11 EU countries, was introduced in January 1999, it marked the start of a unified monetary policy for the euro area under the European Central Bank (ECB). To achieve its ultimate goal of price stability, the ECB adopted a two-pillar strategy.

The first pillar was to set and announce a reference value for year-on-year growth in the M3 money supply. This reference value, which the ECB has published each December since 1998, was initially set and left at 4.5 percent. Three forecasted conditions were assumed in the calculation of this 4.5 percent value: (1) the harmonized index of consumer prices (HICP) for the euro area as a whole would show an inflation rate of less than two percent; (2) economic growth would trend around 2.0 percent–2.5 percent; and (3) the velocity of M3 circulation would fall at a pace of around 0.5 percent–1.0 percent annualized over the medium term.

The second pillar was to assess the risks to price stability. Specifically, the ECB declared that price stability would be defined, in numerical terms, as HICP inflation of less than two percent Y/Y for the euro area over the medium term.

Consider here the intentions behind the ECB's adoption of this two-pillar strategy. First, the ECB maintained that curbing inflation and managing monetary policy with the goal of price stability would bring sustainable employment and income creation over the long term. It also took the stance that money supply was a basic factor behind inflation, and that controlling that supply would be an effective means of achieving price stability over the medium to long term. The ECB thus placed the highest importance on the money supply as an

31

indicator, and released the reference value for the M3 money supply based on the same rationale. Further, the ECB was broadly committed to examining other economic and financial indicators and assessing the outlook for price trends and risks to price stability at the same time.

Later, in May 2003, the ECB revised the framework of its two-pillar strategy for monetary policy. These revisions focused on two points.

First, the ECB announced its intention to keep its effective target for HICP inflation at a level slightly below two percent Y/Y. This was a response to the aggravated deflationary risks spreading throughout the world at the time. The ECB clearly stated, however, that it was neither adopting an inflation target nor applying mechanical policy responses to actual inflation levels. The ECB used the vague expression "medium term" instead of setting a specific target period for price stability. In this sense the ECB differed from the Bank of England, which adopted an inflation target.

Second, the ECB took M3 money supply growth which had been the first pillar of its strategy, and changed it to the second pillar. This was effectively a downgrade of the M3 data in terms of its priority as a policy objective. The actual level of M3 growth had apparently exceeded the 4.5 percent reference value from the time the ECB began managing monetary policy, and from 2001 onward the level deviated upward due to a special factor, namely, the increase of short-term negotiable securities held by non-euro area residents. Put simply, investors shifted from long-term financial products to more liquid short-term financial products amid the deceleration of the global economy. As a result, market confidence in the M3 data dropped sharply and the ECB's emphasis on M3 growth as a policy objective came under mounting criticism.

Note, however, that the ECB kept M3 growth in place as a policy objective in spite of this criticism. To this day, the ECB has apparently been convinced that the trend in the money supply can be taken as a leading indicator of the trend in inflation. From this perspective, a close focus on the M3 money supply trend is important not only for preventing inflation, but also for preempting asset bubbles due to factors such as excess liquidity. In marked contrast with the ECB, the central banks of the US and Japan place little importance on the money supply. They fret that the money supply is too vulnerable to special factors, and that its velocity of circulation lacks transparency.

In this chapter we examine the suitability of the ECB's management of monetary policy with an emphasis on money supply. To do so, we construct an empirical analysis on the stability of the money demand function in the euro area. General stability in the money demand function is an important premise if we are to argue that the money supply has a certain predictable influence on the real economy, or that central bank control of the money supply is effective as a macroeconomic policy. If a stable relationship holds between the real money balance and other variables such as real GDP and interest rates, there should be a stable long-term balance between the nominal money balance and prices.

The stability of the money demand function in the euro area is an important and widely researched topic. Foremost papers have been published by Wesche (1997), Spencer (1997), Fase and Winder (1998), Fagan and Henry (1998), Hayo (1999), and Coenen and Vega (2001). Much of the literature analyzes the stability of the aggregate money demand function in the euro area within a co-integration framework.[1]

This chapter is notable in three ways. First, it analyzes data starting from 1999 when the euro is fully introduced as a common currency. Second, it analyzes the stability of the money demand function for the 11 countries in the euro area, based not only on the standard

---

[1]Wesche (1997), for example, investigates the stability and predictive performance of a European money demand function for M3. Wesche (1997) uses quarterly data on Germany, France, Italy, and the United Kingdom over either of two periods, from 1973 to 1993 for France and Italy, and from 1973 to 1994 for Germany and the United Kingdom. According to the results, the aggregate money demand function seems to mainly reflect the money demand in Germany. This finding gains credence when we note that the European money demand relation becomes unstable if Germany is excluded from the aggregate. Fagan and Henry (1998) empirically analyze the long-run money demand using the EU-wide monetary aggregates composed of four EU countries. Based on the quarterly data between 1981 and 1994, they find that monetary aggregates (M1 and M3) have a co-integrating relation with GDP and interest rates. Hayo (1999) estimates the European money demand for narrow (M1) and broad (M3) money for 11 EMU countries based on quarterly aggregate data from 1964 to 1994. In his calculations, the estimated money demand function is stable for both narrow and broad money. In an analysis with quarterly data from 1980 to 1998, Coenen and Vega (2001) also find a stable money demand model for M3 in the euro area.

co-integration framework for aggregate data, but also on a panel co-integration framework. Nonstationary time series analyses of unit roots, co-integration etc. are known to lack power when the sample sizes are small. This chapter addresses this issue appropriately by panel co-integration methods and then checks the robustness of the empirical results. Third, this chapter checks the robustness of the analytical results using three money supply measures: M1, M2 and M3.[2]

2.2.   Model

Various theories on the money demand function have been proposed. Kimbrough (1986a, 1986b) and Faig (1988), for example, derive the money demand function by explicitly considering transaction costs.

$$\frac{M_t}{P_t} = L(Y_t, R_t) \quad L_Y > 0, \quad L_R < 0, \tag{2.1}$$

where M_t is the nominal money supply for period t; P_t is the price index for period t; Y_t is output for period t; and R_t is the nominal interest rate for period t. Money demand increases when output increases, and decreases when interest rates increase.

We apply two types of specifications corresponding to equation (2.1), as follows:

Model 1:
$$\ln(M_t) - \ln(P_t) = \beta_0 + \beta_1 \ln(Y_t) + \beta_2 R_t + u_{1t}$$
$$\beta_1 > 0, \quad \beta_2 < 0 \tag{2.2}$$

Model 2:
$$\ln(M_t) - \ln(P_t) = \beta_0 + \beta_1 \ln(Y_t) + \beta_2 \ln(R_t) + u_{2t},$$
$$\beta_1 > 0, \quad \beta_2 < 0 \tag{2.3}$$

---

[2] M1 comprises currency, i.e. banknotes and coins, and overnight deposits. M2 comprises M1 and, in addition, deposits with an agreed maturity of up to two years or redeemable at a period of notice of up to and including three months. M3 comprises M2 and certain debt instruments of the resident MFI (Monetary Financial Institutions) sector, namely those used in repurchase agreements, money market fund shares/units and debt securities with a maturity of up to and including two years (including money market paper). (*Source*: http://www.oenb.at/en/geldp_ volksw/ geldpolitik/strategie/eurosystems/ components_of_m3.jsp).

where u_{it} ($i = 1, 2$) is the error term at time t with zero mean and finite variance. Equation (2.2) uses the level of interest rates and equation (2.3) uses the logarithmic value of interest rates. Otherwise, the two equations are the same.

2.3. Aggregate Data Analysis

2.3.1. *Data*

The European Union introduced the euro in January 1999. We therefore set the sample period from that month through to December 2007. We begin here by conducting an empirical analysis with aggregate data from the euro area.

Three types of money supply data are examined: M1, M2 and M3. The ECB uses M3 as the reference value for its monetary policy. Here, however, we use all three variables in order to analyze the stability of the money demand function from a broader perspective. Each type of money supply is seasonally adjusted by X12. The overnight call rate is used for interest rate data, the harmonized index of consumer prices (HICP) is used for prices, the industrial production (IP; seasonally adjusted) index is used as a proxy variable for economic activity, and logarithmic values are used for money supply, price levels, and IP indices. Interest rates are analyzed by two methods, one which takes a logarithm and one which does not. Nominal money balances are deflated by the HICP. The data are taken from the *International Financial Statistics* (International Monetary Fund). Figure 2.1 indicates the movements of the logs of real M1, M2 and M3. All three types of money move upward, and M2 moves almost in parallel with M3.

As a preliminary analysis, we check whether each variable has a unit root or not. According to the augmented Dickey–Fuller test and Philips–Perron test for aggregate data (Dickey and Fuller, 1979; Phillips and Perron, 1988), the null hypothesis of a unit root is accepted for each variable and rejected for the first difference of each variable. Thus, we find that each variable is a I(1) variable with a unit root.

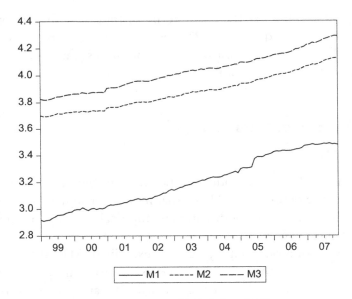

Fig. 2.1. Logs of M1, M2 and M3.

2.3.2. *Demand for M1*

First, we analyze the money demand function in relation to the use of M1 by conducting the Johansen-type co-integration test developed by Johansen (1991) and Johansen and Juselius (1990). Two types of Johansen tests are available: the trace test and the maximum eigenvalue test. In the Johansen-type co-integration test, empirical results depend heavily on the VAR system lag order. Here we confirm the robustness of our empirical results by examining them in two cases, when the lag order is first and when the lag order is second.

Tables 2.1 and 2.2 indicate the results of the co-integration tests for the system $(\ln[M1_t] - \ln[P_t], \ln[Y_t], R_t)$ and system $(\ln[M1_t] - \ln[P_t], \ln[Y_t], \ln[R_t])$, where $M1_t$ is the nominal balance of M1 at time t. The system $(\ln[M1_t] - \ln[P_t], \ln[Y_t], R_t)$ and system $(\ln[M1_t] - \ln[P_t], \ln[Y_t], \ln[R_t])$ correspond to Model 1 and Model 2 respectively.

Table 2.1 indicates the results of the co-integration tests for the system $(\ln[M1_t] - \ln[P_t], \ln[Y_t], R_t)$. Under the null hypothesis of no co-integrating vector, the trace test statistic and its p-value are 40.968

Table 2.1. Johansen-type Co-integration Tests, M1
System: $\ln(M1_t) - \ln(P_t)$, $\ln(Y_t)$, R_t.

H_0	Trace test	p-value	Maximum eigenvalue test	p-value
Lag length = 1.				
$r = 0$	40.968	0.002	31.705	0.001
$r \leq 1$	9.263	0.342	8.481	0.332
Lag length = 2.				
$r = 0$	34.858	0.012	24.831	0.014
$r \leq 1$	10.027	0.279	9.760	0.228

Note: r is the number of co-integrating vectors.

Table 2.2. Johansen-type Co-integration Tests, M1
System: $\ln(M1_t) - \ln(P_t)$, $\ln(Y_t)$, $\ln(R_t)$.

H_0	Trace test	p-value	Maximum eigenvalue test	p-value
Lag length = 1.				
$r = 0$	31.230	0.034	21.956	0.038
$r \leq 1$	9.273	0.341	8.173	0.361
Lag length = 2.				
$r = 0$	28.864	0.064	20.233	0.066
$r \leq 1$	8.631	0.401	8.196	0.359

Note: r is the number of co-integrating vectors.

and 0.002 when the lag length is equal to one, and 34.858 and 0.012 when the lag length is equal to two. The maximum eigenvalue test statistic and its p-value are 31.705 and 0.001 when the lag length is equal to one, and 24.831 and 0.014 when the lag length is equal to two. As this table shows, the null hypothesis is rejected for every case at the five percent significance level. Under the null hypothesis of one co-integrating vector, the trace test statistic and its p-value are 9.263 and 0.342 when the lag length is equal to one, and 10.027 and 0.279 when the lag length is equal to two. The maximum eigenvalue test statistic and its p-value are 8.481 and 0.332 when the lag length is equal to one, and 9.760 and 0.228 when the lag length is equal to two. Here, the null hypothesis is accepted for every case at the conventional significance level. Thus, the existence of a co-integrating relation is supported.

Table 2.2 indicates the results of co-integration tests for the system $(\ln[M1_t] - \ln[P_t], \ln[Y_t], \ln[R_t])$. Under the null hypothesis of no co-integrating vector, the trace test statistic and its p-value are 31.230 and 0.034 when the lag length is equal to one, and 28.864 and 0.064 when the lag length is equal to two. The maximum eigenvalue test statistic and its p-value are 21.956 and 0.038 when the lag length is equal to one, and 20.233 and 0.066 when the lag length is equal to two. The null hypothesis is rejected in two out of four cases at the five percent significance level and in all cases at the 10 percent significance level. Under the null hypothesis of one co-integrating vector, the trace test statistic and its p-value are 9.237 and 0.341 when the lag length is equal to one, and 8.631 and 0.401 when the lag length is equal to two. The maximum eigenvalue test statistic and its p-value are 8.173 and 0.361 when the lag length is equal to one, and 8.196 and 0.359 when the lag length is equal to two. The null hypothesis is accepted for every case at the conventional significance level. In this case we also find evidence to support the existence of a co-integrating relation.

Having thus supported the co-integrating relation, we go on to estimate the money demand function. In estimating the co-integrating vector, the endogeneity for the regressors prevents us from applying the ordinary least squares method. To work our way around this problem, we apply the dynamic ordinary least squares method (DOLS) developed by Stock and Watson (1993). The co-integrating vector is thus estimated by adding $\Delta\ln(Y_t)$, ΔR_t, and their leads and lags in Model 1, and by adding $\Delta\ln(Y_t)$, $\Delta\ln(R_t)$ and their leads and lags in Model 2, as follows:

$$\ln(M1_t) - \ln(P_t) = \beta_0 + \beta_1 \ln(Y_t) + \beta_2 R_t$$

Model 1:
$$+ \sum_{i=-K}^{K} \Delta\ln(Y_{t-i})$$

$$+ \sum_{i=-K}^{K} \Delta R_{t-i} + \nu_{1t}, \qquad (2.4)$$

$$\ln(M1_t) - \ln(P_t) = \beta_0 + \beta_1\ln(\Upsilon_t) + \beta_2\ln(R_t)$$

Model 2:
$$+ \sum_{i=-K}^{K} \Delta\ln(\Upsilon_{t-i})$$

$$+ \sum_{i=-K}^{K} \ln(\Delta R_{t-i}) + v_{2t}. \quad (2.5)$$

where Δ is the difference operator, i.e., $\Delta x_t = x_t - x_{t-1}$.

Table 2.3 shows the estimation results for Model 1 and Model 2. Here, the sign condition of the money demand function clearly holds for all cases. The estimated output coefficients are significant, at positive values of 4.159 and 4.203 for Model 1, and 4.166 and 4.256 for Model 2. The estimated interest rate coefficients are also significant, at negative values of -0.078 and -0.072 for Model 1, and -0.235

Table 2.3. Dynamic OLS, M1.

$$\ln(M1_t) - \ln(P_t) = \beta_0 + \beta_1\ln(\Upsilon_t) + \beta_2 R_t$$

Model 1:
$$+ \sum_{i=-K}^{K} \Delta\ln(\Upsilon_{t-i}) + \sum_{i=-K}^{K} \Delta R_{t-i} + v_{1t}$$

$$\ln(M1_t) - \ln(P_t) = \beta_0 + \beta_1\ln(\Upsilon_t) + \beta_2\ln(R_t)$$

Model 2:
$$+ \sum_{i=-K}^{K} \Delta\ln(\Upsilon_{t-i}) + \sum_{i=-K}^{K} \ln(\Delta R_{t-i}) + v_{2t}$$

Model	K	$\hat{\beta}_1$	$\hat{\beta}_2$	$\bar{R}^2$
Model 1	3	4.159**	−0.078**	0.989
		(52.143)	(−14.602)	
	6	4.203**	−0.072**	0.990
		(50.992)	(−16.745)	
Model 2	3	4.166**	−0.235**	0.981
		(42.235)	(−10.976)	
	6	4.256**	−0.214**	0.985
		(42.882)	(−13.579)	

Note: Numbers in parentheses are t-values.
** shows significance at the one percent level.

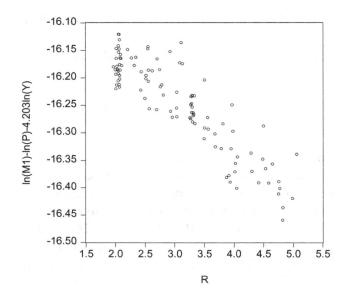

Fig. 2.2.   Scatter Plot of $\ln(M1_t) - \ln(P_t) - 4.203\ln(Y_t)$, R_t.

and -0.214 for Model 2. When using the interest rate in logarithm, the interest rate coefficient of money demand tends to have a higher absolute value.

Figures 2.2 and 2.3 are scatter plots of the system $(\ln[M1_t] - \ln[P_t] - 4.203\ln[Y_t], R_t)$ and system $(\ln[M1_t] - \ln[P_t] - 4.256\ln[Y_t], \ln[R_t])$, respectively. Note that 4.203 and 4.256 are output elasticity estimated by DOL for $K = 6$ in Table 2.3. According to these plots, the demand for M1 looks stable over the sample period for both cases.

As the above results clearly reveal, the calculations with aggregate data for the euro area support a co-integrating relation and the existence of a money demand function with respect to M1.

2.3.3. *Demand for M2*

Next we consider the money demand function when using M2 for the money supply component. Table 2.4 indicates the results of

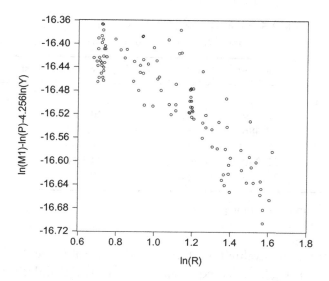

Fig. 2.3. Scatter Plot of $\ln(M1_t) - \ln(P_t) - 4.256\ln(Y_t), \ln(R_t)$.

Table 2.4. Johansen-type Co-integration Tests, M2
System: $\ln(M2_t) - \ln(P_t), \ln(Y_t), R_t$.

H_0	Trace test	p-value	Maximum eigenvalue test	p-value
Lag length = 1.				
$r = 0$	53.414	0.000	42.702	0.000
$r \leq 1$	10.711	0.230	7.488	0.433
Lag length = 2.				
$r = 0$	45.732	0.000	31.627	0.001
$r \leq 1$	14.105	0.080	9.138	0.275

Note: r is the number of co-integrating vectors.

Johansen-type co-integration tests for the system ($\ln[M2_t] - \ln[P_t], \ln[Y_t], R_t$), where $M2_t$ is the nominal balance for M2 at time t. Under the null hypothesis of no co-integrating vector, the trace test statistic and its p-value are 53.414 and 0.000 when the lag length is equal to one, and 45.732 and 0.000 when the lag length is equal to two.

Table 2.5. Johansen-type Co-integration Tests, M2
System: $\ln(M2_t) - \ln(P_t)$, $\ln(Y_t)$, $\ln(R_t)$.

H_0	Trace test	p-value	Maximum eigenvalue test	p-value
Lag length $= 1$.				
$r = 0$	40.099	0.002	30.412	0.002
$r \leq 1$	9.686	0.306	7.199	0.466
Lag length $= 2$.				
$r = 0$	37.050	0.006	24.584	0.016
$r \leq 1$	12.466	0.136	9.011	0.285

Note: r is the number of co-integrating vectors.

The maximum eigenvalue test statistic and its p-value are 42.702 and 0.000 when the lag length is equal to one, and 31.627 and 0.001 when the lag length is equal to two. Thus, the null hypothesis is rejected in all cases at the one percent significance level. Under the null hypothesis of one co-integrating vector, the trace test statistic and its p-value are 10.711 and 0.230 when the lag length is equal to one, and 14.105 and 0.080 when the lag length is equal to two. The maximum eigenvalue test statistic and its p-value are 7.488 and 0.433 when the lag length is equal to one, and 9.138 and 0.275 when the lag length is equal to two. Thus, the null hypothesis may be accepted.

Table 2.5 shows the results of Johansen-type co-integration tests for the system $(\ln[M2_t] - \ln[P_t], \ln[Y_t], \ln[R_t])$. As this table clearly shows, the null hypothesis of no co-integrating relation is rejected in all cases at the five percent significance level, and the null hypothesis of one co-integrating relation is accepted in all cases at the conventional significance level. Thus, the existence of a co-integrating relation is clearly supported.

Having thus supported the co-integrating relation, we go on to estimate the money demand function using DOLS. Table 2.6 shows the estimation results for Model 1 and Model 2. Here, the sign condition of the money demand function holds for all cases. The estimated output coefficients are significant, at positive values of 2.859 and 2.851 for

Table 2.6.   Dynamic OLS, M2.

$$\ln(M2_t) - \ln(P_t) = \beta_0 + \beta_1 \ln(Y_t) + \beta_2 R_t$$

Model 1:
$$+ \sum_{i=-K}^{K} \Delta\ln(Y_{t-i}) + \sum_{i=-K}^{K} \Delta R_{t-i} + \nu_{1t}$$

$$\ln(M2_t) - \ln(P_t) = \beta_0 + \beta_1 \ln(Y_t) + \beta_2 \ln(R_t)$$

Model 2:
$$+ \sum_{i=-K}^{K} \Delta\ln(Y_{t-i}) + \sum_{i=-K}^{K} \ln(\Delta R_{t-i}) + \nu_{2t}$$

Model	K	$\hat{\beta}_1$	$\hat{\beta}_2$	$\bar{R}^2$
Model 1	3	2.859**	−0.043**	0.988
		(42.717)	(−12.469)	
	6	2.851**	−0.041**	0.991
		(45.103)	(−19.339)	
Model 2	3	2.874**	−0.129**	0.979
		(35.543)	(−9.055)	
	6	2.907**	−0.116**	0.985
		(44.054)	(−17.630)	

Note: Numbers in parentheses are t-values.
**shows significance at the one percent level.

Model 1, and 2.874 and 2.907 for Model 2. The estimated interest rate coefficients are also significant, at negative values of −0.043 and −0.041 for Model 1, and −0.129 and −0.116 for Model 2. As seen in Tables 2.3 and 2.6, the estimated elasticity of demand with respect to output is greater for M1 than for M2. We also find that the estimated interest rate coefficient for M1 has a higher absolute value than that for M2.

Figures 2.4 and 2.5 are scatter plots of the system $(\ln[M2_t] - \ln[P_t] - 2.851\ln[Y_t], R_t)$ and system $(\ln[M2_t] - \ln[P_t] - 2.907 \ln[Y_t], \ln[R_t])$ respectively. Note that 2.851 and 2.907 are output elasticities estimated by DOLS for $K = 6$ in Table 2.6. The money demand function for M2 looks stable over the sample period for both cases here as well.

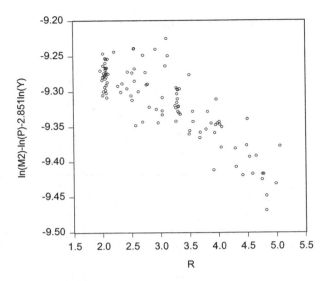

Fig. 2.4.   Scatter Plot of $\ln(M2_t) - \ln(P_t) - 2.851\ln(\Upsilon_t)$, R_t.

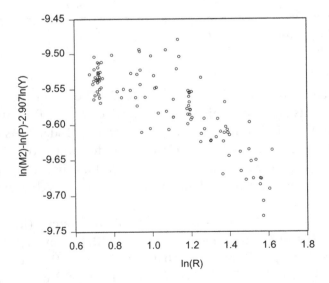

Fig. 2.5.   Scatter Plot of $\ln(M2_t) - \ln(P_t) - 2.907\ln(\Upsilon_t)$, $\ln(R_t)$.

As these results show, the calculations with aggregate data for the euro area support a co-integrating relation and the existence of a money demand function with respect to M2.

2.3.4. *Demand for M3*

Finally, we analyze the money demand function in relation to M3, the money supply component used by the ECB as a reference value in managing monetary policy. Table 2.7 shows the results of Johansen-type co-integration tests for the system $(\ln[M3_t] - \ln[P_t], \ln[Y_t], R_t)$, where $M3_t$ is the nominal balance of M3 at time t. As Table 2.7 shows, the null hypothesis of no co-integrating relation is rejected in all cases at the one percent significance level, and the null hypothesis of one co-integrating relation is accepted in all cases at the conventional significance level. Table 2.8 indicates the results of Johansen-type co-integration tests for the system $(\ln[M3_t] - \ln[P_t], \ln[Y_t], \ln[R_t])$. Here, the null hypothesis of no co-integration is rejected in all cases at the five percent significance level and the null hypothesis of one co-integration is accepted in all cases at the conventional significance level. Thus, we find similar evidence to support the existence of a co-integrating relation.

Having thus supported the co-integrating relation, we go on to estimate the demand function using the DOLS. Table 2.9 shows the estimation results for Model 1 and Model 2. Here, the sign condition of

Table 2.7. Johansen-type Co-integration Tests, M3
System: $\ln(M3_t) - \ln(P_t), \ln(Y_t), R_t$.

H_0	Trace test	p-value	Maximum eigenvalue test	p-value
Lag length = 1.				
$r = 0$	59.303	0.000	50.577	0.000
$r \leq 1$	8.726	0.391	7.055	0.483
Lag length = 2.				
$r = 0$	38.652	0.004	28.473	0.004
$r \leq 1$	10.179	0.267	7.671	0.413

Note: r is the number of co-integrating vectors.

Table 2.8.   Johansen-type Co-integration Tests, M3
System: $\ln(M3_t) - \ln(P_t)$, $\ln(Y_t)$, $\ln(R_t)$.

H_0	Trace test	p-value	Maximum eigenvalue test	p-value
Lag length $= 1$.				
$r = 0$	43.016	0.001	35.423	0.000
$r \leq 1$	7.592	0.510	6.079	0.603
Lag length $= 2$.				
$r = 0$	30.193	0.045	21.921	0.039
$r \leq 1$	8.272	0.437	5.932	0.622

Note: r is the number of co-integrating vectors.

Table 2.9.   Dynamic OLS, M3.

Model 1:
$$\ln(M3_t) - \ln(P_t) = \beta_0 + \beta_1 \ln(Y_t) + \beta_2 R_t$$
$$+ \sum_{i=-K}^{K} \Delta\ln(Y_{t-i}) + \sum_{i=-K}^{K} \Delta R_{t-i} + v_{1t}$$

Model 2:
$$\ln(M3_t) - \ln(P_t) = \beta_0 + \beta_1 \ln(Y_t) + \beta_2 \ln(R_t)$$
$$+ \sum_{i=-K}^{K} \Delta\ln(Y_{t-i}) + \sum_{i=-K}^{K} \ln(\Delta R_{t-i}) + v_{2t}$$

Model	K	$\hat{\beta}_1$	$\hat{\beta}_2$	$\bar{R}^2$
Model 1	3	3.015**	−0.048**	0.986
		(38.776)	(−12.550)	
	6	2.980**	−0.045**	0.989
		(39.733)	(−20.921)	
Model 2	3	3.030**	−0.142**	0.977
		(34.765)	(−9.163)	
	6	3.056**	−0.127**	0.984
		(42.312)	(−18.487)	

Note: Numbers in parentheses are t-values.
**shows significance at the one percent level.

the money demand function holds for all cases. The estimated output coefficients are significant, at positive values of 3.015 and 2.980 for Model 1, and 3.030 and 3.056 for Model 2. The estimated interest rate coefficients are also significant, at negative values of -0.048 and -0.045 for Model 1, and -0.142 and -0.127 for Model 2. As seen in Tables 2.3 and 2.9, the estimated elasticity of demand with respect to output is greater for M1 than for M3. We also find that the estimated interest rate coefficient for M1 has a higher absolute value than that for M3.

Figures 2.6 and 2.7 are scatter plots of the system $(\ln[M3_t] - \ln[P_t] - 2.980\ln[Y_t], R_t)$ and system $(\ln[M3_t] - \ln[P_t] - 3.056\ln[Y_t], \ln[R_t])$, respectively. Note that 2.980 and 3.056 are output elasticity estimated by DOL for $K = 6$ in Table 2.9. The money demand function for M3 looks stable over the sample period for both cases here as well.

As the above results show, the calculations with aggregate data for the euro area support a co-integrating relation and the existence of a money demand function with respect to M3.

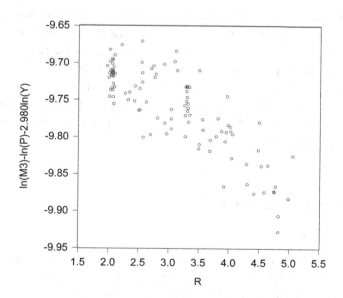

Fig. 2.6.   Scatter Plot of $\ln(M3_t) - \ln(P_t) - 2.980\ln(Y_t), R_t$.

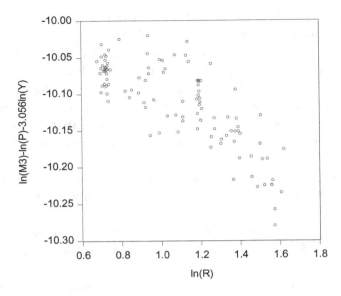

Fig. 2.7. Scatter Plot of $\ln(M3_t) - \ln(P_t) - 3.056\ln(Y_t), \ln(R_t)$.

In summary, our empirical results support the co-integrating relation of money demand for M1, M2, and M3 when using aggregate data of the euro area. Intriguingly, the estimated elasticity of demand with respect to output is greater for M1 than for M2 or M3, and the absolute value of the estimated interest rate coefficient is greater for M1 than for M2 or M3. This suggests that the ECB could reasonably contemplate the use of M1 or M2 as its reference value for managing monetary policy, instead of M3.

2.4. Panel Data Analysis

2.4.1. *Data*

Next, we conduct an empirical analysis with panel data of 11 countries (Austria, Belgium, Finland, France, Germany, Ireland, Italy, Luxembourg, Netherlands, Portugal, and Spain) over the period from January 1999 through December 2007.

Three types of money supply data are examined: M1, M2 and M3. Each type of money supply is seasonally adjusted using X12. The overnight call rate is used for interest rate data, the harmonized index of consumer prices (HICP) of each country is used for prices, the industrial production (IP; seasonally adjusted) index of each country is used as a proxy variable for economic activity, and logarithmic values are used for money supply, price levels, and IP indices. Interest rates are analyzed by two methods, one which takes a logarithm and one which does not.

As a preliminary analysis, we check whether each variable has a unit root or not. According to the panel unit root test developed by Im, Pesaran and Shin (2003) and Levin, Lin and Chu (2002), the null hypothesis of a unit root is accepted for each variable and rejected for the first difference of each variable. Thus, we find that each variable is a I(1) variable with a unit root.

2.4.2. *Demand for M1*

First, we analyze the money demand function in relation to the use of M1 by conducting the Johansen-type panel co-integration test developed by Maddala and Wu (1999) for the money demand function of the 11 countries. Fisher (1932) derives a combined test based on the results of the individual independent tests. Maddala and Wu (1999) use Fisher's result to propose an approach for testing for co-integration in panel data by combining tests from individual cross-sections to obtain a test statistic for the full panel. Two kinds of Johansen-type test are available: The Fisher test from the trace test and the Fisher test from the maximum eigenvalue test. In the Johansen-type panel co-integration test, empirical results depend heavily on the lag order of the VAR system. Here we confirm the robustness of our empirical results by examining them in two cases, when the lag order is first and when the lag order is second. If p_i is the p-value from an individual co-integration test for cross-section i, then under the null hypothesis for the panel, $-2\sum_{i=1}^{N} \log(p_i)$ has an asymptotic chi-square distribution with degrees of freedom equal to $2N$, where N is the number of cross-sections.

Table 2.10.   Johansen-type Panel Co-integration Tests, M1
System: $\ln(M1_t) - \ln(P_t), \ln(Y_t), R_t$.

H_0	Fisher Statistic from trace test	p-value	Fisher Statistic from maximum-eigenvalue test	p-value
Lag length = 1.				
$r = 0$	90.640	0.000	104.300	0.000
$r \leq 1$	15.540	0.838	14.140	0.897
Lag length = 2.				
$r = 0$	57.060	0.000	54.030	0.000
$r \leq 1$	21.570	0.486	23.700	0.363

Note: r is the number of co-integrating vectors.

Table 2.10 gives the results of the panel co-integration tests for the system $(\ln[M1_t] - \ln[P_t], \ln[Y_t], R_t)$. Under the null hypothesis of no co-integrating vector, the Fisher statistic from the trace test and its p-value are 90.640 and 0.000 when the lag length is equal to one, and 57.060 and 0.000 when the lag length is equal to two. The Fisher statistic from the maximum eigenvalue test and its p-value are 104.300 and 0.000 when the lag length is equal to one, and 54.030 and 0.000 when the lag length is equal to two. As this table shows, the null hypothesis is rejected for every case at the one percent significance level. Under the null hypothesis of one co-integrating vector, the Fisher statistic from the trace test and its p-value are 15.540 and 0.838 when the lag length is equal to one, and 21.570 and 0.486 when the lag length is equal to two. The Fisher statistic from the maximum eigenvalue test and its p-value are 14.140 and 0.897 when the lag length is equal to one, and 23.700 and 0.363 when the lag length is equal to two. Here, the null hypothesis is accepted for every case at the conventional significance level. Thus, the existence of a co-integrating relation is supported.

Table 2.11 gives the results of panel co-integration tests for $(\ln[M1_t] - \ln[P_t], \ln[Y_t], \ln[R_t])$. Under the null hypothesis of no co-integrating vector, the Fisher statistic from the trace test and its p-value are 80.970 and 0.000 when the lag length is equal to one, and 50.060

Table 2.11. Johansen-type Panel Co-integration Tests, M1
System: $\ln(M1_t) - \ln(P_t), \ln(Y_t), \ln(R_t)$.

H_0	Fisher Statistic from trace test	p-value	Fisher Statistic from maximum-eigenvalue test	p-value
Lag length $= 1$.				
$r = 0$	80.970	0.000	91.520	0.000
$r \leq 1$	17.440	0.739	14.860	0.868
Lag length $= 2$.				
$r = 0$	50.060	0.001	48.050	0.001
$r \leq 1$	19.790	0.596	21.040	0.519

Note: r is the number of co-integrating vectors.

and 0.001 when the lag length is equal to two. The Fisher statistic from the maximum eigenvalue test and its p-value are 91.520 and 0.000 when the lag length is equal to one, and 48.050 and 0.519 when the lag length is equal to two. Here, the null hypothesis is rejected for every case at the one percent significance level. Under the null hypothesis of one co-integrating vector, the Fisher statistic from the trace test and its p-value are 17.440 and 0.739 when the lag length is equal to one, and 19.790 and 0.596 when the lag length is equal to two. The Fisher statistic from the maximum eigenvalue test and its p-value are 14.860 and 0.868 when the lag length is equal to one, and 21.040 and 0.519 when the lag length is equal to two. The null hypothesis is accepted for every case at the conventional significance level. In this case we also find evidence to support the existence of a co-integrating relation.

Having thus supported the co-integrating relation, we go on to estimate the co-integrating vector. When making this estimation for panel data, the endogeneity for the regressors prevents us from using the ordinary least squares (OLS) method. To work our way around this problem, we apply the fully modified ordinary least squares (panel FMOLS) proposed by Pedroni (2001).[3] Table 2.12 shows the

---

[3]For details on the panel FMOLS, see Appendix A.

Table 2.12. Fully Modified OLS for Panel Data, M1.

Model 1: $\ln(M1_t) - \ln(P_t) = \beta_0 + \beta_1\ln(Y_t) + \beta_2 R_t + u_{1t}$

Model 2: $\ln(M1_t) - \ln(P_t) = \beta_0 + \beta_1\ln(Y_t) + \beta_2\ln(R_t) + u_{2t}$

	$\hat{\beta}_1$	$t(\hat{\beta}_1)$	$\hat{\beta}_2$	$t(\hat{\beta}_2)$
Model 1	3.13**	57.14	−0.06**	−14.75
Model 2	3.05**	54.89	−0.16**	−13.58

Note: ** shows significance at one percent level.

estimation results for Model 1 and Model 2. Here, the sign condition of the money demand function holds for all cases. The estimated output coefficients are significant, at positive values of 3.13 for Model 1 and 3.05 for Model 2. The estimated interest rate coefficients are also significant, at negative values of −0.06 for Model 1 and −0.16 for Model 2. When we use the interest rate in logarithm, the absolute value of the interest rate coefficient tends to be higher.

As the above results show, the analysis with panel data for the euro area support a co-integrating relation and statistically support the existence of a money demand function with respect to M1. These results are consistent with those obtained with the aggregate data.

2.4.3. *Demand for M2*

Next we considered the money demand function when using M2 for the money supply component. Table 2.13 gives the results of panel co-integration tests for the system $(\ln[M2_t] - \ln[P_t], \ln[Y_t], R_t)$. Under the null hypothesis of no co-integrating vector, the Fisher statistic from the trace test and its p-value are 102.200 and 0.000 when the lag length is equal to one, and 72.380 and 0.000 when the lag length is equal to two. The Fisher statistic from the maximum eigenvalue test and its p-value are 116.100 and 0.000 when the lag length is equal to one, and 62.680 and 0.000 when the lag length is equal to two. Thus, the null hypothesis is rejected in all cases at the one percent significance level. Under the null hypothesis of one co-integrating vector, the Fisher

Table 2.13. Johansen-type Panel Co-integration Tests, M2
System: $\ln(M2_t) - \ln(P_t), \ln(Y_t), R_t$.

H_0	Fisher Statistic from trace test	p-value	Fisher Statistic from maximum-eigenvalue test	p-value
Lag length = 1.				
$r = 0$	102.000	0.000	116.100	0.000
$r \le 1$	15.160	0.856	13.810	0.908
Lag length = 2.				
$r = 0$	72.380	0.000	62.680	0.000
$r \le 1$	30.710	0.102	22.060	0.456

Note: r is the number of co-integrating vectors.

statistic from the trace test and its *p*-value are 15.160 and 0.856 when the lag length is equal to one, and 30.710 and 0.102 when the lag length is equal to two. The Fisher statistic from the maximum eigenvalue test and its *p*-value are 13.810 and 0.908 when the lag length is equal to one, and 22.060 and 0.456 when the lag length is equal to two. Thus, the null hypothesis is accepted at the conventional significance level.

Table 2.14 gives the results of panel co-integration tests for the system $(\ln[M2_t] - \ln[P_t], \ln[Y_t], \ln[R_t])$. As this table clearly shows, the null hypothesis of no co-integrating relation is rejected in all cases at the one percent significance level, and the null hypothesis of one co-integrating relation is accepted in all cases at the conventional significance level. The existence of a co-integrating relation is clearly supported.

Having thus supported the co-integrating relation, we go on to estimate the demand function using panel FMOLS. Table 2.15 shows the estimation results for Model 1 and Model 2. Here, the sign condition of the money demand function holds for all cases. The estimated output coefficients are significant, at positive values of 2.07 for Model 1 and 2.03 for Model 2. The estimated interest rate coefficients are also significant, at negative values of −0.03 for Model 1 and −0.08 for Model 2. As Tables 2.12 and 2.15 show, the estimated

Table 2.14.   Johansen-type Panel Co-integration Tests, M2
System: $\ln(M2_t) - \ln(P_t)$, $\ln(Y_t)$, R_t.

H_0	Fisher Statistic from trace test	p-value	Fisher Statistic from maximum-eigenvalue test	p-value
Lag length = 1.				
$r = 0$	87.260	0.000	103.000	0.000
$r \leq 1$	14.330	0.889	13.650	0.913
Lag length = 2.				
$r = 0$	64.710	0.000	59.140	0.000
$r \leq 1$	26.360	0.237	20.650	0.542

Note: r is the number of co-integrating vectors.

Table 2.15.   Fully Modified OLS for Panel Data, M2.

Model 1: $\ln(M2_t) - \ln(P_t) = \beta_0 + \beta_1\ln(Y_t) + \beta_2 R_t + u_{1t}$
Model 2: $\ln(M2_t) - \ln(P_t) = \beta_0 + \beta_1\ln(Y_t) + \beta_2\ln(R_t) + u_{2t}$

	$\hat{\beta}_1$	$t(\hat{\beta}_1)$	$\hat{\beta}_2$	$t(\hat{\beta}_2)$
Model 1	2.07**	(47.14)	−0.03**	(−9.57)
Model 2	2.03**	(45.75)	−0.08**	(−8.44)

Note: **shows significance at the one percent level.

elasticity of demand with respect to output is greater for M1 than for M2. We also find that the estimated interest rate coefficient for M1 has a higher absolute value than that for M2.

As the above results reveal, the calculations with panel data for the euro area support a co-integrating relation and statistically support the existence of a money demand function with respect to M2.

2.4.4.   *Demand for M3*

Finally, we analyze the money demand function in relation to the use of M3, the money supply component used by the ECB as a reference value for managing monetary policy. Table 2.16 gives the results of panel co-integration tests for the system $(\ln[M3_t] - \ln[P_t], \ln[Y_t], R_t)$. As the table clearly shows, the null hypothesis of no co-integrating relation is rejected in all cases at the one percent significance level, and the null hypothesis of one co-integrating relation is accepted in all cases at the conventional significance level. Table 2.17 gives the results of panel co-integration tests for the system $(\ln[M3_t] - \ln[P_t], \ln[Y_t], \ln[R_t])$. The null hypothesis of no co-integration is rejected in all cases at

Table 2.16. Johansen-type Panel Co-integration Tests, M3 System: $\ln(M3_t) - \ln(P_t), \ln(Y_t), R_t$.

H_0	Fisher Statistic from trace test	p-value	Fisher Statistic from maximum-eigenvalue test	p-value
Lag length $= 1$.				
$r = 0$	104.000	0.000	124.100	0.000
$r \leq 1$	9.737	0.989	7.680	0.998
Lag length $= 2$.				
$r = 0$	56.700	0.000	54.350	0.000
$r \leq 1$	21.400	0.496	15.200	0.854

Note: r is the number of co-integrating vectors.

Table 2.17. Johansen-type Panel Co-integration Tests, M3 System: $\ln(M3_t) - \ln(P_t), \ln(Y_t), \ln(R_t)$.

H_0	Fisher Statistic from trace test	p-value	Fisher Statistic from maximum-eigenvalue test	p-value
Lag length $= 1$.				
$r = 0$	89.140	0.000	111.700	0.000
$r \leq 1$	8.733	0.995	6.797	0.999
Lag length $= 2$.				
$r = 0$	47.790	0.001	49.980	0.001
$r \leq 1$	16.910	0.768	11.900	0.960

Note: r is the number of co-integrating vectors.

Table 2.18.   Fully Modified OLS for Panel Data, M3.

Model 1: $\ln(M3_t) - \ln(P_t) = \beta_0 + \beta_1\ln(Y_t) + \beta_2 R_t + u_{1t}$

Model 2: $\ln(M3_t) - \ln(P_t) = \beta_0 + \beta_1\ln(Y_t) + \beta_2\ln(R_t) + u_{2t}$

	$\hat{\beta}_1$	$t(\hat{\beta}_1)$	$\hat{\beta}_2$	$t(\hat{\beta}_2)$
Model 1	2.25**	(46.46)	−0.03**	(−9.27)
Model 2	2.21**	(45.36)	−0.09**	(−8.23)

Note: **shows significance at one percent level.

the one percent significance level and the null hypothesis of one co-integration is accepted in all cases at the conventional significance level. Thus, we find similar evidence to support the existence of a co-integrating relation in this case as well.

Having thus supported the co-integrating relation, we go on to estimate the demand function using the panel FMOLS. Table 2.18 shows the estimation results for Model 1 and Model 2. Here, the sign condition of the money demand function holds for all cases. The estimated output coefficients are significant, at positive values of 2.25 for Model 1 and 2.21 for Model 2. The estimated interest rate coefficients are also significant, at negative values of −0.03 for Model 1 and −0.09 for Model 2. As seen in Tables 2.12 and 2.18, the estimated elasticity of demand with respect to output is greater for M1 than for M3. We also find that the estimated interest rate coefficient for M1 has a higher absolute value than that for M3.

As the above results show, the analysis with panel data for the euro area support a co-integrating relation and statistically support the existence of a money demand function with respect to M3.

In summary, the empirical results of our analysis with panel data of the euro area support the co-integrating relation of money demand for M1, M2, and M3. We note, with interest, that the estimated elasticity of demand for M2 with respect to output is similar to that for M3 but smaller than that for M1. Furthermore, the estimated interest rate coefficient for M2 is similar to that for M3 but smaller than that for

Table 2.19.   Summary of Estimation Results.

Model 1: $\ln(M_t) - \ln(P_t) = \beta_0 + \beta_1 \ln(Y_t) + \beta_2 R_t + u_{1t}$

Model 2: $\ln(M_t) - \ln(P_t) = \beta_0 + \beta_1 \ln(Y_t) + \beta_2 \ln(R_t) + u_{2t}$

		Aggregate data		Panel data	
		$\hat{\beta}_1$	$\hat{\beta}_2$	$\hat{\beta}_1$	$\hat{\beta}_2$
M1	Model 1	4.159	−0.078	3.13	−0.06
		4.203	−0.072		
	Model 2	4.166	−0.235	3.05	−0.16
		4.256	−0.214		
M2	Model 1	2.859	−0.043	2.07	−0.03
		2.851	−0.041		
	Model 2	2.874	−0.129	2.03	−0.08
		2.907	−0.116		
M3	Model 1	3.015	−0.048	2.25	−0.03
		2.980	−0.045		
	Model 2	3.030	−0.142	2.21	−0.09
		3.056	−0.127		

M1, in absolute value. These results (summarized in Table 2.19) are consistent with those using the aggregate data for the euro area.

This suggests that the ECB could reasonably contemplate the use of M1 or M2 as its reference value for managing monetary policy, instead of M3.

2.5.   Some Concluding Remarks

This chapter analyzes the stability of the money demand function using both aggregate data and panel data from January 1999 through December 2007 in the euro area. The analysis leaves us with three important empirical results:

(1) When using aggregate data, we find that the money demand remains stable over the sample period with respect not only to M3, but also to M1 and M2.

(2) When using panel data, the model recognizes the stability of the money demand function over the sample period with respect not only to M3, but also to M1 and M2.
(3) The elasticities of demand for M2 and M3 with respect to output are estimated to be similar to each other, but smaller than the elasticity of demand for M1. Further, the absolute values of the estimated interest rate coefficients for M2 and M3 are similar to each other, but smaller than that for M1.

When the ECB was originally established, it was modeled after Deutsche Bundesbank, the central bank of Germany. In adopting M3 growth as its reference value, the ECB may have been following the example of Deutsche Bundesbank which had been publishing M3 growth as its target. However, the empirical results in this chapter fail to show any particular basis for selecting M3 as a money supply measure. The evidence suggests that the ECB should consider adopting M1 or M2 growth as a reference value, depending on how conditions change in the days to come.[4]

---

[4]This chapter is partly based on Hamori and Hamori (2008a).

Monetary Policy Rule of the European Central Bank

3.1. Introduction

This chapter empirically analyzes the monetary policy rule of the European Central Bank (ECB) from 1999 to 2007. Specifically, we attempt to elucidate how the ECB reacts to changes in economic conditions based on Taylor (1993). The Taylor rule specifies that the central bank sets its instrument, the interest rate, in response to two key target variables: the deviation of contemporaneous inflation from its target value and the deviation of real output from its long-run potential level.

The modeling of the reaction function of central banks has attracted increasing attention from macroeconomists. Analyses of reaction functions may provide background information for future policy decisions by illustrating how interest rates have been set in the past. They also can be useful for capturing the main considerations underlying the rate setting by a central bank.

The Taylor rule is expressed as follows:

$$r_t = b_0 + b_1\pi_t + b_2 y_t, \quad b_1 > 0, \quad b_2 > 0, \qquad (3.1)$$

where r_t, π_t and y_t are the nominal interest rate, inflation rate, and output gap, respectively, at time t. According to this rule, both b_1 and b_2 should both be positive. Thus, a relatively high interest rate should be set when inflation is above its target or when the economy is above its potential level, and a relatively low interest rate should be set when inflation is below its target or when the economy is below its potential level.

Clarida *et al.* (2000) demonstrate the relative accuracy of the Taylor rule in describing how US monetary policy has actually been conducted. Similar observations have been made about central banks in other developed economies (Bernanke and Mihov, 1997; Clarida *et al.*, 1998; Gerlach and Schnabel, 2000; and Gerdesmeier and Roffia, 2003). Indeed, many economists cite the Taylor rule as an important factor behind the success of the central banks in containing inflation and maintaining relative stability in the developed economies since the 1980s.

Gerdesmeier and Roffia (2003), among others, empirically analyze the performance of the Taylor rule and investigate whether the rule can be improved by considering additional economic variables for the euro area. Specifically, they estimate the model using the generalized method of moments (GMM) from January 1985 to February 2002. According to their analysis, a simple model that relates the short-term interest rate to its past values, inflation, and output gap fits the data from the euro area well. They also find that the deviation of the M3 growth rate from its reference value (denoted as a money growth gap) is a significant explanatory variable for interest rates in the euro area.

The research by Gerdesmeier and Roffia (2003) on the euro area is flawed, however, as it ignores the non-stationarity of the data. Kristen (2003) works around the problem by taking a co-integration approach to capture the movements of short-term interest rates in the euro area. In analyses by Kristen (2003) with quarterly data from the first quarter of 1988 to the second quarter of 2002, a model augmented by long-term interest rates yields a stable reaction function.

This chapter empirically analyzes the Taylor rule for the euro area with monthly data from January 1999 to December 2007. We start with a brief explanation of the theoretical background of the simple Taylor rule. Next, we empirically analyze whether the Taylor rule applies to the euro area as a co-integrating relation-ship among the short-term interest rate, inflation rate, and output gap. Last, we analyze the role of the long-term interest rate as an additional explanatory variable for the Taylor rule, as suggested by Kristen (2003).

3.2. The Taylor Rule

Svensson (1997) and Ball (1999) derive the Taylor rule based on the optimization behavior of the central bank. They do so within the framework of inflation targeting, a policy approach characterized by three properties: (a) an announced numerical inflation target, (b) inflation-forecast targeting (a monetary policy heavily reliant on inflation forecasts), and (c) high levels of transparency and account-ability (Svensson, 2007).

Svensson (1997) takes up the case where the central bank has set a long-run inflation target (π^*) but no long-run output target (other than the natural rate of output), as monetary policy is incapable of affecting output in the long run. Suppose, in the short run, that the goal of monetary policy is to stabilize inflation and output around the long-run inflation target and natural output level respectively. The monetary policy thus seeks a symmetry between inflation and output in the short run, but not in the long run. We can describe the relationship as follows, with a period loss function:

$$L\left(\pi_t, y_t\right) = \frac{1}{2}\left[\left(\pi_t - \pi^*\right)^2 + \theta y_t^2\right], \quad \theta > 0, \qquad (3.2)$$

where θ is a relative weight on output stabilization.

We describe the economy with two equations. The first is the aggregate-spending equation:

$$y_{t+1} = \alpha_1 y_t + \alpha_2(r_t - \pi_t) + u_{1,t+1}, \quad \alpha_1 > 0, \ \alpha_2 < 0, \qquad (3.3)$$

where y_t, r_t, π_t and u_{1t} are the gap between output and potential output, the nominal interest rate, the inflation rate, and a white noise shock, respectively, at time t. In Equation (3.3), a rise in the interest rate reduces output with a one-period lag. Output also depends on lagged output, which means that we have persistence. The shock u_{1t} captures other influences on spending such as consumer confidence and fiscal policy.

The second equation is the accelerationist Phillips curve:

$$\pi_{t+1} = \pi_t + \gamma y_t + u_{2,t+1}, \quad \gamma > 0, \qquad (3.4)$$

where u_{2t} is a white noise shock. In Equation (3.4), the change in inflation depends on the output gap in the previous period. The shock u_{2t} is an inflation or supply shock triggered by a big event such as a large movement of oil prices.

Suppose that the central bank's objective in period t is to choose a sequence of current and future interest rates so as to minimize the inter-temporal loss function given by

$$E_t \sum_{\tau=t}^{\infty} \beta^{\tau-t} L\left(\pi_t, y_t\right), \qquad (3.5)$$

where $E_t(\bullet)$ denotes expectations conditional upon (the central bank's) information variable in period t, β is the discount factor fulfilling $0 < \beta < 1$, and $L\left(\pi_t, y_t\right)$ is the period loss function expressed by Equation (3.2). Thus, we can interpret the interest rate in the model as short term. In other words, the central bank wishes to minimize the expected sum of two discounted future deviations: that of inflation from the target and that of output from its natural level.

In Svensson (1997), the solution of this problem yields the following policy reaction function:[1]

$$i_t = \pi_t + a_1(\pi_t - \pi^*) + a_2 y_t. \qquad (3.6)$$

The interest rate increases when current inflation exceeds the inflation target, and also when the output gap widens.

Alternatively, we have

$$i_t = b_0 + b_1 \pi_t + b_2 y_t, \quad b_1 > 0, \quad b_2 > 0, \qquad (3.7)$$

where $b_0 = -a_1 \pi^*$, $b_1 = 1 + a_1$, and $b_2 = a_2$. Equation (3.7) corresponds to the Taylor-type policy response function of Equation (3.1).

---

[1] Note that

$$a_1 = -\frac{1-c}{a_2 \gamma}, \quad a_2 = -\frac{1-c+a_1}{\alpha_2}, \quad c = \frac{\theta}{\theta + \beta \gamma^2 k},$$

and

$$k = \frac{1}{2}\left[1 - \frac{\theta(1-\beta)}{\beta \gamma^2} + \sqrt{\{1 + \theta(1-\beta)/\beta\gamma^2\}^2 + \frac{4\theta}{\gamma^2}}\right] \geq 1.$$

3.3. Data

We perform the empirical analysis with monthly data from January 1999 to December 2007. This sample period can be assumed to be meaningful, as the ECB begins implementing a unified monetary policy in January 1999.

The overnight call rate is used as the short-term interest rate, the government bond yield is used as the long-term interest rate, the harmonized index of consumer prices (HICP) of the euro area is used for prices, and the industrial production (IP; seasonally adjusted) index of the euro area serves as a proxy variable for economic activity. The data are taken from the *International Financial Statistics* (International Monetary Fund). Figure 3.1 shows the movements of the short-term interest rate. From this pattern, we can conjecture that the ECB carried out a tight monetary policy up to 2001, then shifted to an easy monetary policy.

To obtain the potential output, we regress the output on a constant and a time trend, as follows:

$$\ln(Y_t) = \alpha + \beta \times time + v_t, \tag{3.8}$$

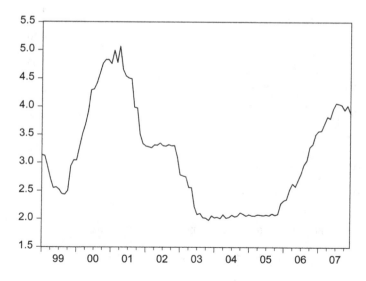

Fig. 3.1.   Short-term Interest Rate.

where Υ_t is the output at time t, *time* is the time trend, and v_t is the error term with mean 0 and finite variance. Next, the potential output is described as the predicted value of Equation (3.8), as follows:

$$\ln(\Upsilon_t^*) = \hat{\alpha} + \hat{\beta} \times time, \tag{3.9}$$

where Υ_t^* is the potential output, and $\hat{\alpha}, \hat{\beta}$ are estimates of α, β.

The output gap, meanwhile, is calculated as the deviation of output from its potential level, as follows:

$$
\begin{aligned}
y_t &= 100 \times \left(\ln(\Upsilon_t) - \ln(\Upsilon_t^*) \right) \\
&= 100 \times \ln \left(1 + \frac{\Upsilon_t - \Upsilon_t^*}{\Upsilon_t^*} \right) \\
&\simeq 100 \times \frac{\Upsilon_t - \Upsilon_t^*}{\Upsilon_t^*},
\end{aligned} \tag{3.10}
$$

where Υ_t is the output at time t, and y_t is the output gap at time t. Figure 3.2 indicates the series of actual output, fitted output, and residuals. The residuals correspond to the output gap.

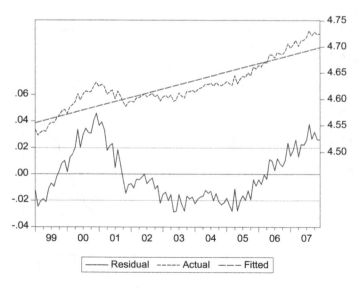

Fig. 3.2.   Actual Output, Fitted Output, and Residuals.

The inflation rate is calculated as the log difference of the HICP from the previous month, as follows:

$$\pi_t = 1200 \times \left(\ln(p_t) - \ln(p_{t-1}) \right)$$

$$= 1200 \times \ln \left(1 + \frac{p_t - p_{t-1}}{p_{t-1}} \right)$$

$$\simeq 1200 \times \frac{p_t - p_{t-1}}{p_{t-1}}, \tag{3.11}$$

where π_t and p_t are the inflation rate and price level respectively at time t.

As a preliminary analysis, we conduct the ADF test (augmented Dickey–Fuller test) developed by Dickey and Fuller (1979) for each variable. We find that the null hypothesis of a unit root tends to be rejected for the level of each variable, and that the null hypothesis of a unit root is rejected for the first difference of each variable. Thus, each variable is likely to be a I(1) variable with a unit root.

3.4. Empirical Results

3.4.1. *Simple Taylor Rule*

First, we analyze the simple Taylor rule, Equation (3.1), using the monthly data over the period from January 1999 to December 2007. Specifically, we conduct two Johansen-type co-integration tests for the policy reaction function (Johansen, 1991; and Johansen and Juselius, 1990): the trace test and the maximum eigenvalue test.

Table 3.1 presents the results of the co-integration tests. Because the Johansen test depends on the lag order, we use alternative lag orders, i.e., three and six periods, to examine the robustness of the test results. Under the null hypothesis of no co-integration, the trace test statistic and its p-value are 71.860 and 0.000 when the lag length is equal to three, and 36.978 and 0.000 when the lag length is equal to six. The maximum eigenvalue test statistic and its p-value are 55.397 and 0.000 when the lag length is equal to three, and 27.753 and 0.000 when lag length is equal to six. As the table shows, the null hypothesis is rejected

Table 3.1.   Co-integration Test: (r_t, π_t, y_t).

Lag	Null hypothesis	Trace test	Maximum eigenvalue test
3	$r = 0$	71.860 (0.000)	55.397 (0.000)
6	$r = 0$	36.978 (0.006)	27.753 (0.005)

Note: r is the hypothesized number of co-integrating equations. The numbers in parentheses are p-values.

in all cases at the one percent significance level. Thus, there is likely to be a co-integrating relationship among the interest rate, inflation rate, and output gap.

Having thus supported the existence of the co-integrating relation, we go on to estimate the Taylor rule. When estimating the co-integrating vector, the endogeneity for the regressors prevents us from using the ordinary least squares method. To work our way around this problem, we apply the dynamic ordinary least squares method (DOLS) developed by Stock and Watson (1993). The co-integrating vector in Equation (3.7) is estimated by adding $\Delta \pi_t$, Δy_t, and their leads and lags as follows:

$$r_t = b_0 + b_1 \pi_t + b_2 y_t + \sum_{i=-K}^{K} \gamma_{ri} \Delta \pi_{t-i} + \sum_{i=-K}^{K} \gamma_{yi} \Delta y_{t-i} + \varepsilon_t, \quad (3.12)$$

where Δ is the difference operator, i.e., $\Delta x_t = x_t - x_{t-1}$, and ε_t is the error term.

The estimation results are presented in Table 3.2. As the table shows, the output coefficient is estimated to be positive (0.472 for $K = 3$ and 0.502 for $K = 6$) and statistically significant in all cases at the one percent level. The inflation coefficient is also estimated to be positive (0.021 for $K = 3$ and 0.113 for $K = 6$), but not to a statistically significantly degree in any case.

Table 3.2. Dynamic OLS.

$$r_t = b_0 + b_1 \pi_t + b_2 y_t + \sum_{i=-K}^{K} \gamma_{ri} \Delta \pi_{t-i} + \sum_{i=-K}^{K} \gamma_{yi} \Delta y_{t-i} + u_t$$

Lead and lag	Variable	Coefficient	SE	t-statistic	p-value	$\bar{R}^2$
$K = 3$	Constant	3.083	0.125	24.732	0.000	0.915
	π_t	0.021	0.056	0.374	0.710	
	y_t	0.472	0.024	20.082	0.000	
$K = 6$	Constant	2.897	0.345	8.404	0.000	0.934
	π_t	0.113	0.153	0.736	0.464	
	y_t	0.502	0.030	16.635	0.000	

Note: SE is the Newey-West HAC Standard Error (lag truncation = 5).

3.4.2. *The Role of Long-term Interest Rate*

Our next step is to empirically analyze the role of the long-term interest rate, according to the approach of Kristen (2003). In this section we extend the model by adding the long-term interest rate as an additional explanatory variable as follows:

$$r_t = b_0 + b_1 \pi_t + b_2 y_t + b_3 l_t, \quad b_1 > 0, \quad b_2 > 0, \quad b_3 > 0, \quad (3.13)$$

where l_t is the long-term interest rate at time t.

Here, we conduct Johansen-type co-integration tests for the short-term interest rate, inflation rate, output gap, and long-term interest rate. Table 3.3 shows the results of the co-integration tests. Because the Johansen test depends on the lag order, we use alternative lag orders, i.e., three and six periods, to examine the robustness of the test results. Under the null hypothesis of no co-integration, the trace test statistic and its p-value are 85.067 and 0.000 when the lag length is equal to three, and 61.105 and 0.002 when the lag length is equal to six. The maximum eigenvalue test statistic and its p-value are 52.623 and 0.000 when the lag length is equal to three, and 28.665 and 0.036 when the lag length is equal to six. As this table shows, the null hypothesis of no co-integrating relation is rejected in three out of four cases at the one percent level and in all cases at the five percent level. Thus, there

Table 3.3.   Co-integration Test: (r_t, π_t, y_t, l_t).

Lag	Null hypothesis	Trace test	Maximum eigenvalue test
3	$r = 0$	85.067	52.623
		(0.000)	(0.000)
6	$r = 0$	61.105	28.665
		(0.002)	(0.036)

Note: r is the hypothesized number of co-integrating equations.
The numbers in parentheses are p-values.

is likely to be a co-integrating relationship among the interest rate, inflation rate, output gap, and long-term interest rate.

Having thus supported the existence of the co-integrating relation, we estimate the extended Taylor rule using DOLS. The co-integrating vector in Equation (3.12) is estimated by adding $\Delta\pi_t$, Δy_t, Δl_t, and their leads and lags as follows:

$$r_t = b_0 + b_1\pi_t + b_2 y_t + b_3 l_t$$
$$+ \sum_{i=-K}^{K} \gamma_{ri}\Delta\pi_{t-i} + \sum_{i=-K}^{K} \gamma_{yi}\Delta y_{t-i} + \sum_{i=-K}^{K} \gamma_{li}\Delta l_{t-i} + w_t,$$
$$(3.14)$$

where w_t is the error term.

The estimation results are presented in Table 3.4. As the table shows, the output coefficient is estimated to be positive (0.414 for $K = 3$ and 0.454 for $K = 6$) and statistically significant in all cases at the one percent level. The inflation rate coefficient is also estimated to be positive (0.031 for $K = 3$ and 0.010 for $K = 6$), but not to a statistically significantly degree in any case. The coefficient of the long-term interest rate is estimated to be positive (0.304 for $K = 3$ and 0.293 for $K = 6$) and statistically significant in all cases at the one percent level. These results are consistent with Kristen (2003) and confirm the importance of the long-term interest rate in the analysis of the policy reaction function.

Table 3.4. Dynamic OLS.

$$r_t = b_0 + b_1\pi_t + b_2 y_t + b_3 l_t + \sum_{i=-K}^{K} \gamma_{ri}\Delta\pi_{t-i}$$

$$+ \sum_{i=-K}^{K} \gamma_{yi}\Delta y_{t-i} + \sum_{i=-K}^{K} \gamma_{li}\Delta l_{t-i} + u_t$$

Lead and lag	Variable	Coefficient	SE	t-statistic	p-value	$\bar{R}^2$
$K = 3$	Constant	1.699	0.346	4.906	0.000	0.946
	π_t	0.031	0.042	0.725	0.471	
	y_t	0.414	0.026	15.860	0.000	
	l_t	0.304	0.070	4.332	0.000	
$K = 6$	Constant	1.791	0.363	4.930	0.000	0.962
	π_t	0.010	0.106	0.091	0.928	
	y_t	0.454	0.027	16.566	0.000	
	l_t	0.293	0.064	4.566	0.000	

Note: SE is the Newey–West HAC Standard Error (lag truncation = 5).

3.5. Some Concluding Remarks

This chapter empirically analyzes the Taylor-type policy response function of the ECB using monthly data from January 1999 to December 2007. The empirical results can be summarized as follows:

(1) With the simple Taylor rule, the co-integrating relation among the interest rate, inflation rate, and output gap was empirically supported.
(2) According to the DOLS, the estimated coefficients of output and inflation are both positive, but only the former is statistically significant.
(3) With the extended Taylor rule, the co-integrating relation among the short-term interest rate, inflation rate, output gap, and long-term interest rate was also empirically supported.
(4) The DOLS results indicate that the coefficient of the long-term interest rate is positive and statistically significant.

Kristen (2003) suggests that the long-term interest rate can serve as a proxy for the public perception of the long-run inflation rate. The downward shift in inflationary expectations, for example, will be accompanied by a drop in long-term interest rates. On this basis, we can argue that the interest-setting in the euro area has been forward-looking. Our empirical results are consistent with those of Kristen (2003).

Empirical Analysis of the Term Structure of Interest Rates in the Presence of Cross-Section Dependence

4.1. Introduction

The European Central Bank (ECB) relies on three key interest rates to adjust the operating target (EONIA: Euro Overnight Index Average) to a desirable level: the rate on the main refinancing operations (the MRO minimum bid rate) and the rates on marginal lending facilities and deposit facilities (the two standing facility rates). The marginal lending facility rate and the deposit facility rate serve as upper and lower boundaries for the overnight call rate (the short-term market rate). The role of the main refinancing operations rate is to adjust the central interest rate to a desirable level. On 28 June 2000, the ECB introduced variable rate tenders in the place of fixed rate tenders for the main refinancing operations. Shortly afterwards, the bank also began to announce minimum bid rates as an adjustment to the new tender system.

Monetary policy and fiscal policy are generally viewed as two approaches for macroeconomic stabilization. Central banks are responsible for monetary policy, while governments are responsible for fiscal policy. In the euro area, the ECB oversees a unified monetary policy for the euro area members, while the governments of the member states manage their fiscal policies independently. This leads to a problem with the term structure of interest rates. Short-term interest rates can be controlled to some extent through monetary policy management by the ECB (as described above). Long-term interest rates, meanwhile, fluctuate in response to the fiscal conditions of the member states assessed by factors such as fiscal policy stances and the status of government bond issues. Consequently, the movements of short-term and long-term interest rates can become significantly disjointed. The EU and ECB are both aware of this problem.

To uphold faith in the single currency, the Stability and Growth Pact concluded by the EU member states sets forth rules for the promotion of fiscal discipline in the countries that have adopted the euro. If these rules are effective, one would expect to observe consistency in the movements of short-term and long-term interest rates. If, on the other hand, the rules are ineffective and individual governments implement fiscal policies tailored to their own fiscal situations, one would expect the movements of the short-term and long-term interest rates to be inconsistent with each other. This chapter examines this point through an expectation-theory-based empirical analysis of the term structure of interest rates.

The term structure of interest rates is the interaction between the short-term interest rates of bonds of different maturities, or the interactions between short-term and long-term interest rates. Economists and policymakers pay close attention to the term structure of interest rates when setting monetary policy. The expectations hypothesis (EH) is one of the several equilibrium theory hypotheses used to explain the empirically observed co-movement of yields of securities with different maturities. The EH holds that interest rates for securities of different maturities should not, on average, deviate from each other to a large degree. In other words, the EH suggests that the long-term interest rate is an average of the expected future short-term rates, plus a time-independent term premium. The movements in interest rates within the term structure have a common stochastic trend that drives this movement in the long run. The contending hypothesis, known as the segmented market hypothesis, suggests that each interest rate is determined by its own forcing variables.

Many investigators have recognized the importance of the expectations theory and examined it by empirical analyses (Choi and Wohar, 1991; Zhang, 1993; Hardouvelis, 1994; Siklos and Wohar, 1996; Gerlach and Smets, 1997; Kugler, 1997; Bekaert and Hodrick, 2001; King and Kurmann, 2002; Tillman, 2006; Hamori and Hamori, 2008b).

To treat this subject from a different approach, this chapter applies a non-stationary panel data analysis to the euro area member states. Specifically, we consider the cross-section dependence among variables. The ECB began managing monetary policy in earnest in 1999 when the euro was introduced. With a small sample size, it would be difficult to apply an ordinary time-series analysis. To overcome this small-sample problem, we carry out a series of analyses using a panel of 11 countries, i.e., Austria, Belgium, Finland, France, Germany, Ireland, Italy, Luxembourg, the Netherlands, Portugal, and Spain.[1] In our analysis of the term-structure of interest rates, the short-term interest is the common variable among the countries in the euro area. To prevent this from creating cross-section dependence among the countries in the panel, we apply the approach of Pesaran (2007).

4.2. Model

Following Hall *et al.* (1992), we state the expectation hypothesis in general, as follows:

$$R(n)_t = \frac{1}{n} \sum_{j=0}^{n-1} E_t[R(1)_{t+j}] + L(n), \qquad (4.1)$$

where $R(n)_t$ represents the continuously compounded yield to maturity of an n-period long-term bond and $R(1)_{t+j}$ represents the short-term interest rate for n successive periods. $E_t[\bullet]$ denotes the expectations operator conditioned on the information available at time t, and $L(n)$ is the term premium. The term premium measures the additional gain from holding long-term bonds relative to rolling over one-period bonds. Equation (1) shows that in achieving equilibrium yields, an investor is indifferent between holding a discount bond with n-periods to maturity and investing in another one-period bond for n-successive periods, plus a term premium.

---

[1] As McDonald (1996, p. 9) points out, statistical power can be improved dramatically by carrying out a unit-root test on a pooled set of cross-section data rather than performing separate unit-root tests for individual series.

Rearranging equation (1), we obtain the yield spread as follows:

$$S(n)_t = R(n)_t - R(1)_t = \frac{1}{n}\sum_{j=1}^{n-1}\sum_{i=1}^{j} E_t \Delta R(1)_{t+i} + L(n), \quad (4.2)$$

where $S(n)_t$, the yield spread, is $R(n)_t - R(1)_t$.

When, for example, $n = 1$ in equation (4.1), we obtain:

$$R(2)_t = \frac{1}{2}\left[R(1)_t + E_t R(1)_{t+1}\right] + L(2). \quad (4.3)$$

By rearranging equation (4.3), we obtain,

$$S(2)_t = R(2)_t - R(1)_t = \frac{1}{2}\left[E_t R(1)_{t+1} - R(1)_t\right] + L(2), \quad (4.4)$$

which corresponds to equation (4.2).

Similarly, when $n = 2$ in equation (4.1), we obtain:

$$R(3)_t = \frac{1}{3}\left[E_t R(1)_t + E_t R(1)_{t+1} + E_t R(1)_{t+2}\right] + L(3). \quad (4.5)$$

By rearranging equation (4.3), we obtain,

$$\begin{aligned}
S(3)_t &= R(3)_t - R(1)_t \\
&= \frac{1}{3}\left[E_t R(1)_{t+1} - R(1)_t + E_t R(1)_{t+2} - E_t R(1)_{t+1}\right. \\
&\quad \left. + E_t R(1)_{t+1} - R(1)_t\right] + L(3),
\end{aligned} \quad (4.6)$$

which corresponds to equation (4.2).

If $R(n)_t$ and $R(1)_t$ are integrated processes with a unit root, then $S(n)_t$ becomes stationary. The expectation hypothesis asserts that there should be co-integrating vectors of the form $(1, -1)$, such that $R(n)_t$ is co-integrated with $R(1)_t$ over the long run. Though deviations from the equilibrium condition occur in the short run, portfolio adjustments by investors in reaction to this disequilibrium will effectively restore the equilibrium in the long run. Thus, testing for a co-integrating relationship between $R(n)_t$ and $R(1)_t$ is effectively the same as testing for unit roots in a yield spread.

4.3. Data

Figure 4.1 shows the movements of the long-term government yield and short-term interest rate in the aggregate euro area from January 1999 to December 2007. The money market rate and long-term government yield in the euro area are used as the short-term interest rate and long-term interest rate respectively. The data are taken from the *International Financial Statistics* (International Monetary Fund). As the figure indicates, the long-term interest rate is higher than the short-term interest rate during this period, but the difference between the rates changes over the business cycles. The short-term interest rate approaches the long term interest rate in around 2000, but then starts to deviate.

The empirical analysis of this chapter is carried out with the panel data of 11 countries (Austria, Belgium, Finland, France, Germany, Ireland, Italy, Luxembourg, the Netherlands, Portugal, and Spain)

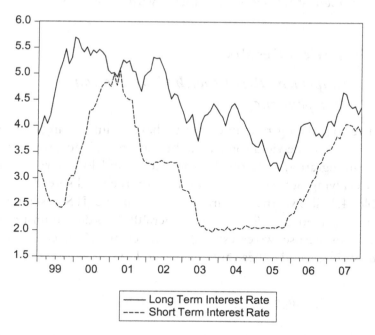

Fig. 4.1. Long-Term and Short-Term Interest Rates in the Euro Area.

from January 1999 to December 2007. The euro was introduced in January 1999. We therefore set the sample period from that month through to December 2007. The overnight money market rate is used as the short-term interest rate, and is a common variable for each country. Government bond yields are used for the long-term rates, and vary from country to country.

As a preliminary analysis, we check whether each variable has a unit root or not. For long-term interest rates, we carry out panel unit root tests such as those from Levin, Lin, and Chu test; Im, Pesaran, and Shin (IPS) test; the ADF–Fisher chi-square test; and the PP–Fisher chi-square test (Levin *et al.*, 2002; Im *et al.*, 2003; Maddala and Wu, 1999). For the short-term interest rate, we carry out the augmented Dickey–Fuller test and Philips–Perron test (Dickey and Fuller, 1979; Phillips and Perron, 1988). As a result, we find that the null hypothesis of a unit root is accepted for the level of each variable and rejected for the first difference of each variable. Thus, each of the long-term and short-term interest rates is a I(1) variable with a unit root.

4.4.   Empirical Results

4.4.1.   *Empirical Results with Cross-Section Independence*

If short-term and long-term interest rates have co-integrating vectors of the form (1,–1), the yield spread will be stationary. Thus, we perform panel co-integration tests on the short-term and long-term interest rates by carrying out panel unit-root tests on the yield spreads.

Table 4.1 shows the empirical results of the IPS tests for 11 countries from January 1991 to December 2007. As deterministic term specifications, we use two cases: (1) fixed effect, and (2) fixed effect and individual time trend. These are given as follows:

$$\Delta y_{it} = a_i + b_i y_{i,t-1} + \sum_{j=1}^{p} c_{ij} \Delta y_{i,t-j} + u_{it},$$

$$i = 1, 2, \ldots, N; \quad t = 1, 2, \ldots, T \qquad (4.7)$$

Table 4.1.   Panel Unit Root Tests.
Panel A: With Fixed Effect

	$p = 0$	$p = 1$
IPS	-0.129	-1.227

Panel B: With Fixed Effect and Time Trend

	$p = 0$	$p = 1$
IPS	0.608	-0.278

Note: IPS is the standardized *t*-bar test statistic from Im *et al.* (2003).

and

$$\Delta y_{it} = a_{0i} + a_{1i}t + b_i y_{i,t-1} + \sum_{j=1}^{p} c_{ij}\Delta y_{i,t-j} + u_{it},$$

$$i = 1, 2, \ldots, N; \quad t = 1, 2, \ldots, T \quad (4.8)$$

where t is the time trend, u_{it} is the error term of i-th cross section at time t, and Δ is the difference operator, i.e., $\Delta y_{it} = y_{it} - y_{i,t-1}$. Equations (4.7) and (4.8) give the standard ADF(p) regression with a constant term and with a constant term and time trend, respectively, where p is the lag length of the augmented term in ADF regression.

The null hypothesis is that the yield spreads have unit roots (there is no co-integrating relationship between short-term and long-term interest rates). The alternative hypothesis is that the yield spreads do not have unit roots (there is a co-integrating relationship between short-term and long-term interest rates). We choose the lag length for the auxiliary regression as one ($p = 0$) and two ($p = 1$) and use the Bertlett kernel for the Newey–West bandwidth.

With fixed effects, the test statistic is -0.129 for $p = 0$ and -1.227 for $p = 1$. With fixed effects and individual time trends, the test statistic is 0.608 for $p = 0$ and -0.278 for $p = 1$. In summary, the null hypothesis of no co-integration is not rejected in any case at the five percent significance level. This means that the yield spreads are nonstationary variables with a unit root, and hence that short-term and long-term interest rates have no co-integrating relationships with a co-integrating vector of the form $(1,-1)$. Our empirical results, therefore, do not support the expectation hypothesis for the international term structure of interest rates in the euro area.

4.4.2. Empirical Results with Cross-Section Dependence

Panel unit root tests can lead to spurious results if they fail to take account of significant degrees of positive error cross-section dependence. The problem can be quite serious when the cross-section dependence is high. It thus becomes important to check the degree of residual cross-section dependence.

We estimate individual ADF(p) regressions without cross-section augmentations for $p = 0$ and $p = 1$, then compute pair-wise cross-section correlation coefficients of the residuals from these regressions ($\hat{\rho}_{ij}$). Tables 4.2, 4.3, 4.4, and 4.5 indicate the results for the case of the ADF(0) regressions with intercept, the ADF(1) regressions with intercept, the ADF(0) regressions with intercept and trend, and the ADF(1) regressions with intercept and trend. As the tables show, the pair-wise correlation is greater than 0.90 and statistically significant for every case. Thus, the cross-section dependence may be too high.

Table 4.6 gives the simple average of these correlation coefficients across all pairs, $\bar{\rho}$, together with the associated cross-section dependence (CD) test statistic proposed by Pesaran (2004). These are defined as follows:

$$\bar{\rho} = \frac{2}{N(N-1)} \sum_{i=1}^{N-1} \sum_{j=i+1}^{N} \hat{\rho}_{ij}, \qquad (4.9)$$

and

$$CD = \left[\frac{TN(N-1)}{2} \right]^{\frac{1}{2}} \bar{\rho}. \qquad (4.10)$$

As the table shows, the average cross-section error correlation coefficient is around 0.98, and the CD statistics are strongly significant. The results are robust to the choice of lag order (p) and the specification

Table 4.2. Cross Correlation of the Residuals in the ADF(0) Regressions with Intercept.

	Aus	Bel	Fin	Fra	Ger	Ire	Ita	Lux	Net	Por	Spa
Aus	1.00										
	—										
Bel	0.99	1.00									
	(0.00)	—									
Fin	0.98	0.99	1.00								
	(0.00)	(0.00)	—								
Fra	0.99	0.99	0.99	1.00							
	(0.00)	(0.00)	(0.00)	—							
Ger	0.99	0.99	0.99	1.00	1.00						
	(0.00)	(0.00)	(0.00)	(0.00)	—						
Ire	0.98	0.99	0.99	0.99	0.99	1.00					
	(0.00)	(0.00)	(0.00)	(0.00)	(0.00)	—					
Ita	0.99	0.99	0.99	0.99	0.99	0.99	1.00				
	(0.00)	(0.00)	(0.00)	(0.00)	(0.00)	(0.00)	—				
Lux	0.92	0.92	0.91	0.91	0.91	0.91	0.91	1.00			
	(0.00)	(0.00)	(0.00)	(0.00)	(0.00)	(0.00)	(0.00)	—			
Net	0.99	0.99	0.99	1.00	0.99	0.99	0.99	0.91	1.00		
	(0.00)	(0.00)	(0.00)	(0.00)	(0.00)	(0.00)	(0.00)	(0.00)	—		
Por	0.99	0.99	0.99	0.99	0.99	0.99	0.99	0.92	1.00	1.00	
	(0.00)	(0.00)	(0.00)	(0.00)	(0.00)	(0.00)	(0.00)	(0.00)	(0.00)	—	
Spa	0.99	1.00	0.99	1.00	0.99	0.99	0.99	0.92	0.99	0.99	1.00
	(0.00)	(0.00)	(0.00)	(0.00)	(0.00)	(0.00)	(0.00)	(0.00)	(0.00)	(0.00)	—

Note: Numbers in parentheses are the p-values for $H_0 : \rho_{ij} = 0$.

of ADF regressions. Thus, panel unit root tests which allow for cross-section dependence are preferable for our analysis.

Pesaran (2007) augments the standard ADF regressions with the cross-section averages of lagged levels and first differences, as follows:

$$\Delta y_{it} = a_i + b_i y_{i,t-1} + c_i \bar{y}_{t-1}$$
$$+ \sum_{j=0}^{p} d_{ij} \Delta \bar{y}_{t-j} + \sum_{j=1}^{p} \delta_{ij} \Delta y_{i,t-j} + u_{it}, \quad (4.11)$$

Table 4.3. Cross Correlation of the Residuals in the ADF(1) Regressions with Intercept.

	Aus	Bel	Fin	Fra	Ger	Ire	Ita	Lux	Net	Por	Spa
Aus	1.00										
	—										
Bel	0.99	1.00									
	(0.00)	—									
Fin	0.98	0.99	1.00								
	(0.00)	(0.00)	—								
Fra	0.99	0.99	0.99	1.00							
	(0.00)	(0.00)	(0.00)	—							
Ger	0.99	0.99	0.99	1.00	1.00						
	(0.00)	(0.00)	(0.00)	(0.00)	—						
Ire	0.98	0.99	0.99	0.99	0.99	1.00					
	(0.00)	(0.00)	(0.00)	(0.00)	(0.00)	—					
Ita	0.99	0.99	0.99	0.99	0.99	0.99	1.00				
	(0.00)	(0.00)	(0.00)	(0.00)	(0.00)	(0.00)	—				
Lux	0.92	0.91	0.91	0.91	0.91	0.91	0.91	1.00			
	(0.00)	(0.00)	(0.00)	(0.00)	(0.00)	(0.00)	(0.00)	—			
Net	0.98	0.99	0.99	1.00	0.99	0.99	0.99	0.91	1.00		
	(0.00)	(0.00)	(0.00)	(0.00)	(0.00)	(0.00)	(0.00)	(0.00)	—		
Por	0.98	0.99	0.99	0.99	0.99	0.99	0.99	0.92	0.99	1.00	
	(0.00)	(0.00)	(0.00)	(0.00)	(0.00)	(0.00)	(0.00)	(0.00)	(0.00)	—	
Spa	0.98	1.00	0.99	0.99	0.99	0.99	0.99	0.92	0.99	0.99	1.00
	(0.00)	(0.00)	(0.00)	(0.00)	(0.00)	(0.00)	(0.00)	(0.00)	(0.00)	(0.00)	—

Note: Numbers in parentheses are the p-values for $H_0 : \rho_{ij} = 0$.

and

$$\Delta y_{it} = a_{0i} + a_{1i}t + b_i y_{i,t-1} + c_i \bar{y}_{t-1}$$

$$+ \sum_{j=0}^{p} d_{ij} \Delta \bar{y}_{t-j} + \sum_{j=1}^{p} \delta_{ij} \Delta y_{i,t-j} + u_{it}, \qquad (4.12)$$

where $\bar{y}_t = N^{-1} \sum_{j=1}^{N} y_{jt}$. Equations (4.11) and (4.12) give the cross-sectionally augmented DF regression (CADF) with a fixed effect

Table 4.4. Cross Correlation of the Residuals in the ADF(0) Regressions with Intercept and Trend.

	Aus	Bel	Fin	Fra	Ger	Ire	Ita	Lux	Net	Por	Spa
Aus	1.00										
	—										
Bel	0.99	1.00									
	(0.00)	—									
Fin	0.98	0.99	1.00								
	(0.00)	(0.00)	—								
Fra	0.99	0.99	0.99	1.00							
	(0.00)	(0.00)	(0.00)	—							
Ger	0.99	0.99	0.99	1.00	1.00						
	(0.00)	(0.00)	(0.00)	(0.00)	—						
Ire	0.98	0.99	0.99	0.99	0.99	1.00					
	(0.00)	(0.00)	(0.00)	(0.00)	(0.00)	—					
Ita	0.99	0.99	0.99	0.99	0.99	0.99	1.00				
	(0.00)	(0.00)	(0.00)	(0.00)	(0.00)	(0.00)	—				
Lux	0.92	0.92	0.91	0.91	0.91	0.91	0.91	1.00			
	(0.00)	(0.00)	(0.00)	(0.00)	(0.00)	(0.00)	(0.00)	—			
Net	0.98	0.99	0.99	1.00	0.99	0.99	0.99	0.91	1.00		
	(0.00)	(0.00)	(0.00)	(0.00)	(0.00)	(0.00)	(0.00)	(0.00)	—		
Por	0.99	0.99	0.99	0.99	0.99	0.99	0.99	0.92	0.99	1.00	
	(0.00)	(0.00)	(0.00)	(0.00)	(0.00)	(0.00)	(0.00)	(0.00)	(0.00)	—	
Spa	0.99	1.00	0.99	1.00	0.99	0.99	0.99	0.92	0.99	0.99	1.00
	(0.00)	(0.00)	(0.00)	(0.00)	(0.00)	(0.00)	(0.00)	(0.00)	(0.00)	(0.00)	—

Note: Numbers in parentheses are the p-values for $H_0 : \rho_{ij} = 0$.

and with a fixed effect and individual time trend respectively. Thus, the cross-sectionally augmented version of the IPS (CIPS) test statistic is given as follows:

$$CIPS(N, T) = \frac{1}{N} \sum_{i=1}^{N} t_i(N, T), \qquad (4.13)$$

Table 4.5. Cross Correlation of the Residuals in the ADF(1) Regressions with Intercept and Trend.

	Aus	Bel	Fin	Fra	Ger	Ire	Ita	Lux	Net	Por	Spa
Aus	1.00										
	—										
Bel	0.99	1.00									
	(0.00)	—									
Fin	0.98	0.99	1.00								
	(0.00)	(0.00)	—								
Fra	0.99	0.99	0.99	1.00							
	(0.00)	(0.00)	(0.00)	—							
Ger	0.99	0.99	0.99	1.00	1.00						
	(0.00)	(0.00)	(0.00)	(0.00)	—						
Ire	0.98	0.99	0.99	0.99	0.99	1.00					
	(0.00)	(0.00)	(0.00)	(0.00)	(0.00)	—					
Ita	0.99	0.99	0.99	0.99	0.99	0.99	1.00				
	(0.00)	(0.00)	(0.00)	(0.00)	(0.00)	(0.00)	—				
Lux	0.92	0.91	0.91	0.91	0.91	0.91	0.91	1.00			
	(0.00)	(0.00)	(0.00)	(0.00)	(0.00)	(0.00)	(0.00)	—			
Net	0.98	0.99	0.99	1.00	0.99	0.99	0.99	0.91	1.00		
	(0.00)	(0.00)	(0.00)	(0.00)	(0.00)	(0.00)	(0.00)	(0.00)	—		
Por	0.98	0.99	0.99	0.99	0.99	0.99	0.99	0.92	0.99	1.00	
	(0.00)	(0.00)	(0.00)	(0.00)	(0.00)	(0.00)	(0.00)	(0.00)	(0.00)	—	
Spa	0.98	1.00	0.99	0.99	0.99	0.99	0.99	0.92	0.99	0.99	1.00
	(0.00)	(0.00)	(0.00)	(0.00)	(0.00)	(0.00)	(0.00)	(0.00)	(0.00)	(0.00)	—

Note: Numbers in parentheses are the p-values for $H_0 : \rho_{ij} = 0$.

where $t_i(N, T)$ is the cross-sectionally augmented ADF statistic for the i-th cross-section given by the t-ratio of the coefficient of $y_{i,t-1}$ in the CADF regression.

Table 4.7 gives the results of the CIPS test which allows for cross-section dependence. Here, the CIPS test statistic is -2.376 for $p = 0$ and -2.301 for $p = 1$ when each CADF regression includes a fixed effect, and -2.216 for $p = 0$ and -3.247 for $p = 1$ when each CADF regression includes a fixed effect and individual time trend. The null

Table 4.6. Cross-Section Dependence.
Panel A: With Fixed Effect

	$p = 0$	$p = 1$
$\bar{\bar{\rho}}$	0.978	0.977
CD	75.024	74.561

Panel B: With Fixed Effect and Time Trend

	$p = 0$	$p = 1$
$\bar{\bar{\rho}}$	0.978	0.977
CD	75.030	74.571

Note: $\bar{\bar{\rho}}$ is the average of pair-wise cross-section correlation coefficients of the residuals from ADF regression.
CD is the cross-section dependence test statistic proposed by Pesaran (2004).

Table 4.7. Panel Unit Root Tests with Cross-Section Dependence.
Panel A: With Fixed Effect

	$p = 0$	$p = 1$
CIPS	−2.376	−2.301

Panel B: With Fixed Effect and Time Trend

	$p = 0$	$p = 1$
CIPS	−3.216	−3.247

Note: CIPS is the cross-section average of the t-ratio of the OLS coefficient of $y_{i,t-1}$ in the CADF regressions.

hypothesis of a unit root is rejected at the five percent significance level irrespective of the value of the lag length or specification for CADF regressions. Thus, the empirical results contradicting the expectations theory based on the IPS test could be spurious.

4.5.　Some Concluding Remarks

This chapter empirically analyzes the term structure of interest rates in the euro area from January 1999 to December 2007 for 11 countries: Austria, Belgium, Finland, France, Germany, Ireland, Italy, Luxembourg, the Netherlands, Portugal, and Spain. Specifically, we consider the cross-section dependence using the techniques developed by Pesaran (2007). The empirical results can be summarized as follows:

(1) In a non-stationary panel data analysis which disregards the cross-section dependence, the expectations hypothesis does not hold in the euro area.
(2) Because the residual cross-section dependence turns out to be high, panel unit root tests which allow for cross-section dependence are preferable for our analysis.
(3) The expectation hypothesis is compatible with the short-term and long-term interest rate fluctuations in the euro area when the model appropriately accounts for the cross-section dependence. These results also suggest that the fiscal rules in the euro area function well.

The empirical results of our analysis have some policy implications. As in Japan and the US, the governments of euro area countries have the power to impact long-term interest rate fluctuations through their control over fiscal policy and government bond issues. Yet to maintain faith in their single currency, the euro, these governments are legally obligated to follow rules set forth in the Stability and Growth Pact to promote fiscal discipline.

Specifically, these rules require the euro area governments to restrict fiscal deficits to no more than three percent of GDP, to restrict government debt to no more than 60 percent of GDP, and to work over the medium term to achieve balanced budgets or surpluses. The euro area governments must also send the European Commission annual Stabilization Plans with fiscal deficit targets as percentages of their GDPs, and take active steps to achieve those plans. The Economic and Financial Affairs (ECOFIN) Council inspects and monitors Stabilization Plans, and the finance ministers of the euro area countries discuss their fiscal plans in the newly established Economic and Monetary Committee. The President and Vice-President of the European Central Bank are authorized to attend these meetings and to apply pressure on any countries with weak fiscal discipline.

Under the terms of the Stability and Growth Pact, the European Commission issues a warning to any country whose fiscal deficit exceeds three percent of its GDP. Later, if the warning fails to bring about positive action or desired effects, the Council of the European Union imposes a sanction against the country. Under this sanction, the relevant country is required to set aside up to 0.5 percent of its GDP as a non-interest-bearing deposit. If no improvement is made within two years from the date the sanction is imposed, this deposit may be collected as a fine. This sanction is waived if the real annual growth of a country is less than −2 percent.

The Stability and Growth Pact was adopted at the Dublin Summit in December 1996, at the urging of Germany. Yet after the implementation of the monetary union, six (Germany, France, Italy, Holland, Portugal, and Greece) of the 12 countries that had adopted the euro subjected themselves to excessive deficit procedures which pushed their deficits over the three percent limit. Germany was among the six. And by the end of 2005, seven of the euro area countries had government debt in excess of 60 percent of GDP. In March 2005, the EU responded to the situation by loosening the requirements of the Stability and Growth Pact. Specifically, the EMU countries were allowed to exclude the following items from their deficit calculations, among others: R&D expenses, employment promotion costs, pension reform costs, and costs required for exceptional events, such as the reunification of East and West Germany. Through this adjustment of the terms of the Stability and Growth Pact, and with the help of an economic recovery, fiscal conditions in the aforementioned countries have been slowly improving since about 2004, and further improvement is expected. France met the three percent deficit standard in 2005, and Germany is estimated to have met it in 2006. Though monitoring by the European Commission continues, the excessive deficit procedures for France and Germany have been effectively halted.

The results of the empirical analysis discussed in this chapter suggest that the rules on fiscal discipline in the Stability and Growth Pact are functioning well in the euro area. The euro area countries continue to work steadily to abide by these rules, and to cooperatively pursue the monetary policy management of the ECB and the fiscal management policies of their own governments.

Are Budget Deficits Sustainable
in the Euro Area?

5.1. Introduction

In January 1999, 11 of the EU countries adopted the euro as a single currency. From that month onward, the European Central Bank (ECB) began pursuing a unified monetary policy for the euro area. Though authorized to manage monetary policy, the ECB is of course powerless to control the fiscal policies or fiscal situations of EU countries individually. This lack of fiscal control constrains the bank's management of monetary policy to some degree. If fiscal conditions in one euro area country were to significantly worsen, the monetary policy would become all the more difficult for the bank to handle. The Economic and Monetary Union (EMU), the organization of countries that have adopted the euro single currency, limits the risk of this by requiring any state seeking EMU entry to meet certain standards on budget deficits and government debt. Under the Maastricht Treaty (European Union Treaty) signed in February 1992, member states of the European community had to meet the following economic convergence criteria in the third stage of the EMU scheduled to commence on 1 January 1999.

(1) The average consumer price increase during the year preceding the assessment is less than the average for the three EU-members with the lowest consumer price increases, plus 1.5 percent.
(2) The average long-term interest rate during the year preceding the assessment is equal to or less than the average for the three EU-members with the lowest consumer price increases, plus two percent.

(3) The fiscal deficit is not greater than three percent of nominal GDP, or, if close to the three percent ratio, is either effectively and continuously shrinking or at that level on a temporary and exceptional basis.

(4) Government debt is not greater than 60 percent of nominal GDP, or is declining toward the 60 percent ratio at an acceptable rate.

(5) The control rate in foreign exchange markets has not been lowered in response to destabilizing events in the country applying, and the exchange rate of the country's currency has moved only within the range established through the Exchange Rate Mechanism (ERM) for at least the last two years.

The rationale for imposing the requirements was clear. If the monetary union had been implemented without sufficient convergence of the economic conditions in the participating countries, the ECB would have faced significant obstacles in pursuing a unified monetary policy. This, in turn, would have weakened the world's faith in both the ECB and the euro. In later discussions, the Council of EU decided to use the actual figures for 1997 to determine whether individual countries met the conditions for participation in the monetary union. The most difficult conditions to meet, from among the five listed above, were the ceilings on fiscal deficits and government debt. As of 1996, only one of the then 15 EU member states, Luxembourg, met both standards. The steps taken by the other member states to reduce their fiscal deficits were necessarily harsh, but by and large successful: 14 countries had cut their deficits to less than or equal to three percent of GDP as of 1997. Only Greece failed to do so. The situation was different, however, with regard to the standard on government debt. By the same year, only four member states, Luxembourg, France, Finland, and the UK, were within the debt ceiling of less than 60 percent of GDP. The other countries, meanwhile, were judged to be steadily bringing their debt down toward the standard. In deciding which of the countries could participate, political considerations came into play. In the end, the European Council determined, at a special summit held in May 1998 in Brussels, Belgium, that 11 of the 15 EU member states would adopt the euro as a single currency.

The UK, Denmark, and Sweden chose not to participate in the monetary union, and Greece failed to meet all five of the participation conditions.

With the implementation of the monetary union, the ECB and EU recognized that the EMU member countries would have to abide by the rules on fiscal discipline if the ECB's monetary policy and efforts to stabilize the value of the euro were to succeed. This led to the establishment of a regimen of rules on fiscal discipline in the Stability and Growth Pact. The agreement was initially proposed by Germany, which sought strict enforcement of Article 104(c) of the Maastricht Treaty to cope with the emergence of excessive fiscal deficits in monetary union participants. When the agreement was approved by the European Council at the 1996 Dublin Summit, the name of the agreement was changed from the Stability Pact to the Stability and Growth Pact, at the strong insistence of France.

The Stability and Growth Pact has two key points:

(1) Mutual Surveillance Framework for Realizing Sound Fiscal Management.

All EU member states, whether monetary union participants or not, must establish medium-term fiscal targets, enumerate measures for achieving them, and put forth their own fiscal programs for releasing information on their domestic fiscal conditions. The fiscal programs submitted by the member states are reviewed by the European Commission and the Economic and Financial Affairs (ECOFIN) Council, both of which issue early warnings to any country judged to be in danger of incurring an excessive fiscal deficit.

(2) Matters Regarding Rules and Sanction Procedures for Excessive Fiscal Deficits.

An excessive fiscal deficit is basically a deficit of greater than three percent of GDP. If, however, a country with a fiscal deficit is also suffering a recession with economic contraction of two percent or more annually, no sanctions are imposed on that country for the excessive deficit. And in some cases, the ECOFIN Council will even consider requests to waive the sanctions for countries in fiscal deficit with milder economic contractions of less than two percent. To prevent abuse of this rule, the Council will not, in principle, consider such requests unless the economy is contracting by at least 0.75 percent. If the European Commission and the Council of the European Union determine that a deficit of three percent or more is not excessive, they must present a written explanation to higher authorities. Thus, the system is set up to prevent countries from easily evading sanctions.

If the European Commission concludes that a country's fiscal deficit exceeds three percent of GDP, it will prepare an Excessive Deficit Procedure Report on the fiscal situation of that country. The Economic and Monetary Committee (EMC) receives the report and renders its opinion within two weeks. Article 109(c) of the Maastricht Treaty called for the establishment of the EMC as an economic and financial consultative body. The Committee came into being in January 1999, just when the third stage of the EMU commenced. Its members include one representative from the government of each euro area country, one representative from the central bank of each euro area country, two representatives from the ECB, and two representatives from the European Commission. The European Commission considers the opinion of the EMC and submits a report to the ECOFIN Council which, by a majority vote, determines whether the subject country has an excessive deficit. The country in question, meanwhile, is advised to take measures to reduce its deficit. If it fails to do so, the ECOFIN Council imposes, within 10 months of the recommendation for corrective measures, a sanction requiring the country to set aside a non-interest-bearing deposit. If no fiscal improvement is noted within two years, the EU takes the non-interest-bearing deposit as a fine. The non-interest-bearing deposit consists of two portions, a fixed portion (0.2 percent of GDP) and variable portion (1/10 of the deficit in excess of three percent of GDP), which together are not to exceed 0.5 percent of GDP.

If the ECOFIN Council is unable to determine whether the country has an excessive deficit, the European Council will issue a European Council Resolution on the matter. This resolution carries significant weight as political guidance, and the European Council may follow up by issuing another resolution to provide guidance to the ECOFIN Council and the European Commission. Sanction determinations, therefore, can be taken all the way to the European Council, the EU's top decision-making body, through highly political procedures.

To summarize, the rules on fiscal discipline have been kept in place since the euro area participants were first determined, and the ECB is pursuing a unified monetary policy for the euro area now that the single euro currency is established. In this chapter we seek to determine whether the rules on fiscal discipline are functioning or not. Specifically, we empirically analyze whether a euro area country can suffer growing fiscal deficits severe enough to end in fiscal collapse.

Beginning with Hamilton and Flavin (1986) and Wilcox (1989), much research has been done on the very important topic of budget sustainability. With the advance of methods in time-series analysis, co-integrating tests have often been applied. Prime examples of this research include Trehan and Walsh (1988), Hakkio and Rush (1991), Haug (1991), and Ahmed and Rogers (1995).

The co-integrating test has constraints, however, as it relies on the power of the unit root test. And, as is well known, the unit root tests put forth by Dickey and Fuller (1979), Phillips and Perron (1988), and others (or co-integrating tests based on these unit root tests) are much less powerful when the sample sizes are small. This poses a major problem with the use of fiscal data, which tend to be annual since budgets are assembled only once yearly. If a sustainability test based on co-integrating analysis can only be performed with annual data, the sample sizes will be small as a matter of course. A unit root test (or co-integrating test) could therefore indicate, falsely, that a certain variable has a unit root (or has no co-integrating relationship) when in fact it has none (or has a co-integrating relationship).

The chapter contributes in two ways. First, it provides an empirical analysis of budget sustainability in the euro area. A certain level of fiscal discipline is required of any country wishing to adopt the euro single currency and place itself under the unified monetary policy of the ECB. The key objective of this chapter is to test whether the requirements of the euro area improve fiscal performance. The second contribution of this chapter is our use of a panel unit root test to overcome traditional problems in analyzing budget sustainability. This approach implies that we can use a combination of data on multiple countries to perform powerful tests even when our data are limited to annual statistics on individual countries.

5.2.   Model

This section demonstrates the sustainability condition for the government budget constraint, based on the method of Ahmed and Rogers (1995). The government budget constraint for period t is given by:

$$G_t - T_t + r_{t-1}B^g_{t-1} = B^g_t - B^g_{t-1}, \tag{5.1}$$

where B^g_t is government bonds at time t, G_t is government expenditure at time t, T_t is tax revenue at time t, and r_t is the interest rate from t to $t+1$. Equation (5.1) shows that the government budget deficit has to be financed by creating new debt.

Next, the consumer's optimization condition is expressed as:

$$E_t[(1 + r_t)s_{t,t+1}] = 1, \tag{5.2}$$

where $s_{t,t+j}$ is the marginal rate of substitution between consumption in period t and $t+j$.

It follows from equations (5.1) and (5.2) that

$$E_t\left[\sum_{j=0}^{\infty} s_{t,t+j}G_{t,t+j}\right] - E_t\left[\sum_{j=0}^{\infty} s_{t,t+j}T_{t,t+j}\right] + (1 + r_{t-1})B^g_{t-1}$$

$$= \lim_{N \to \infty} E_t\left[s_{t,t+N}B^g_{t+N}\right]. \tag{5.3}$$

When the limit term on the right-hand side of equation (5.3) is equal to zero, the government debt outstanding is equal to the expected present value of the future net surplus. This condition, what some have described as "a no-Ponzi game," rules out the possibility of bubble financing of the economy. Ahmed and Rogers (1995) demonstrate that the currently expected paths of government spending and taxation are sustainable when this condition holds.

If we take the first difference of equation (5.3) and substitute for ΔB^g_{t-1} from equation (5.1), we get

$$
\Delta E_t \left[\sum_{j=1}^{\infty} s_{t,t+j} G_{t+j} \right] - \Delta E_t \left[\sum_{j=1}^{\infty} s_{t,t+j} T_{t+j} \right]
$$
$$
+ \left(G + r_{t-1} B^g_{t-1} - T_t \right) = \lim_{N \to \infty} E_t \left[s_{t,t+N} B^g_{t+N} \right]
$$
$$
- \lim_{N \to \infty} E_{t-1} \left[s_{t-1,t+N-1} B^g_{t+N-1} \right].
$$
(5.4)

Under certain (and plausible) conditions, Ahmed and Rogers (1995) demonstrate that the presence of a co-integrating relationship in $(T_t, G_t, r_{t-1} B^g_{t-1})$ with the co-integration vector $(1, -1, -1)$ is a necessary and sufficient condition for the present-value budget constraint to hold (i.e., the limit term in equation (5.3) is zero, and the two limit terms in equation (5.4) must therefore also be zero).

As equation (5.1) clearly indicates, the co-integrating relation among $(T_t, G_t, r_{t-1} B^g_{t-1})$ with a co-integrating vector of $(1, -1, 1)$ is equivalent to ΔB^g_t being stationary. Thus, the stationarity of ΔB^g_t is the necessary and sufficient condition for the government's present value constraints to be satisfied.

5.3. Data

The tests cover the 11 countries (Austria, Belgium, Germany, Spain, Finland, France, Ireland, Italy, Luxembourg, Netherlands, and Portugal) that have been part of the euro area since the establishment of the ECB. To keep within the constraints of data usability, the analyses are performed based on budget sizes relative to GDP. The data are taken from the ECB homepage. The empirical analysis covers the following two sample periods.[1]

Sample Period A: 1991 to 2005.
Sample Period B: 1997 to 2005.

---

[1] The data for Spain are only applicable for the period beginning in 1995.

Sample Period A is set as 1991 to 2005 to account for the unification of East and West Germany. Sample Period B is set as 1997 to 2005 because participation in the monetary union is determined based on the fiscal conditions for 1997.

5.4.   Empirical Results

The budget deficits of the EU are analyzed by the techniques of the panel unit root test. Levin *et al.* (2002) suggest that individual unit root tests have limited power against alternative hypotheses, especially in small samples. This poses a serious problem for our current analysis, as our data are limited to annual statistics between 1991 and 2005. To overcome the problem, six different panel unit root tests are applied: the Levin, Lin and Chu test; the Im, Pesaran and Shin test; the ADF–Fisher chi-square test; the ADF–Choi test; the PP–Fisher chi-square test; and the PP–Choi test (Levin, Lin and Chu, 2002; Im, Pesaran and Shin, 2003; Maddala and Wu, 1999; Choi, 2001).

If $(T_t, G_t, r_{t-1}B_{t-1}^g)$ is in a co-integrating relationship with a co-integrating vector of the form $(1,-1,1)$, then ΔB_t^g is stationary; and if ΔB_t^g is stationary, the budget is sustainable. On this basis, we analyze the budget sustainability by performing panel unit root tests on government budget deficit.

The deterministic term specification is used as the fixed effect. SBIC is used to select the lag order. The null hypothesis is that government debt has a panel unit root. The alternative hypothesis is that the government budget deficit has no panel unit root.

Table 5.1 presents empirical results for the period 1991 to 2005. The null hypothesis is rejected for only one of the six cases at the one percent significance level, and for three of the six cases at the five percent significance level. Thus, we cannot clearly determine whether budget deficits are stationary variables without unit roots. This may indicate that budget deficits are not necessarily sustainable.

Table 5.2 presents empirical results for the period 1997 to 2005. The null hypothesis is rejected for five of the six cases at the one percent significance level, and for all six cases at the five percent significance level. These results hint, quite strongly, that the government budget

Table 5.1. Panel Unit Root Tests. 1991–2005.

Method	Test-statistic	p-value
Levin, Lin and Chu t test	−2.912	0.002
Im, Pesaran and Shin W test	−1.758	0.039
ADF–Fisher Chi-Square test	30.503	0.107
ADF–Choi Z test	−1.869	0.031
PP–Fisher Chi-Square test	28.466	0.161
PP–Choi Z test	−1.410	0.079

Note: The p-values for Fisher tests are computed with an asymptotic chi-square distribution. All other tests assume asymptotic normality. The ADF–Fisher chi-square and ADF–Choi Z tests show that the individual unit root test is based on ADF–type tests. The PP–Fisher chi-square and PP–Choi Z tests show that the individual unit root test is based on Phillips-Perron-type tests.

Table 5.2. Panel Unit Root Tests. 1997–2005.

Method	Test-statistic	p-value
Levin, Lin and Chu t test	−5.188	0.000
Im, Pesaran and Shin W test	−2.496	0.006
ADF–Fisher Chi-Square test	43.933	0.008
ADF–Choi Z test	−2.995	0.001
PP–Fisher Chi-Square test	40.088	0.011
PP–Choi Z test	−2.598	0.005

Note: The p-values for Fisher tests are computed with an asymptotic chi-square distribution. All other tests assume asymptotic normality. The ADF–Fisher chi-square and ADF–Choi Z tests show that the individual unit root test is based on ADF–type tests. The PP–Fisher chi-square and PP–Choi Z tests show that the individual unit root test is based on Phillips-Perron-type tests.

deficit is sustainable. And notably, we find that the empirical results for Sample B are much clearer than those for Sample A.

We also check the robustness of our results by shifting the beginning of the sample period in one-year increments. Specifically, we analyze the sample periods 1991–2005, 1992–2005, 1993–2005, 1994–2005,

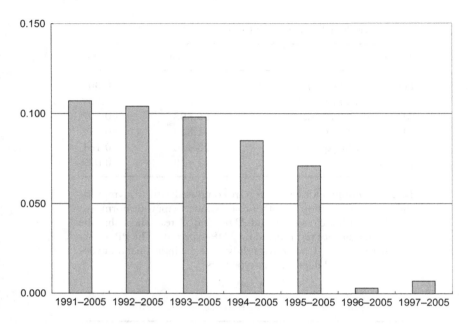

Fig. 5.1.   *P*-values for the ADF–Fisher Chi-Square Tests.

1995–2005, 1996–2005, and 1997–2005, then examine the movement of the test statistics. When the sample period is set to begin around 1997, we find that the budget sustainability is supported at both the one percent and five percent significance levels (see Figure 5.1).

5.5.   Some Concluding Remarks

This chapter empirically examines the issue of budget sustainability for 11 euro area countries. Through this analysis, the fiscal performance of the euro area cannot be clearly confirmed as sustainable or unsustainable from 1991 to 2005. We do find, however, with high certainty, that the fiscal performance is sustainable from 1997 to 2005. This suggests that the rules on fiscal discipline are functioning and that the deficits of the individual countries are steadily shrinking.

That having been said, we add that fundamental changes to the Stability and Growth Pact were accepted at the March 2005 meeting of the European Council in Brussels, mainly at the insistence of France, Germany, and other large countries. Under one of those changes, the excessive deficit determination is waived even for a country with a deficit higher than three percent of GDP, provided that the margin of excess is small and temporary, or that the economic growth rate is either negative or persistently below the potential growth rate. Under another of the changes, the deficit calculations exclude items such as pension reform costs; expenditures on research, development and innovation; and burdens arising from achieving of European policy objectives, notably the process of European unification.[2]

Though the three percent rule has been kept in place, it has been greatly loosened over the years through various provisions to grant exceptions. The time limits for excessive deficit recognition and sanction procedures have also been extended. The ECB and the national central banks of the member countries have argued that these revisions of the Stability and Growth Pact have weakened the rules of fiscal discipline, hindered the policies to promote fiscal strength, and increased the risk of expanding deficits over the medium-to-long term. Expanding or chronic deficits in euro area countries will make it difficult for the ECB to stably manage monetary policy. It remains open to question whether conditions will continue to support the favorable empirical results of our analysis. This will depend on whether the European Commission, European Council, and other institutions and governments from the euro area recognize their responsibilities and successfully apply rules of fiscal discipline to keep sound budgets over the medium term.[3]

---

[2] See Deutsche Bundesbank (2005).
[3] This chapter is based on Hamori and Hamori (2009a).

Yield Spread and Output Growth in the Euro Area

6.1. Introduction

Since the seminal work by Fisher (1907), the relationship between the aggregate economic activity and the yield spread has been one of the most important research topics in financial economics. Harvey (1993, p. 6) provides a general background by explaining the basic mechanism of interaction between the yield spread and aggregate economic activity. Here is an outline of Harvey's analysis. Most consumers prefer a reasonably stable level of income. A volatile level, one which swings from very high to very low through the stages of the business cycle, is generally less attractive to consumers. This preference for stability drives the demand for insurance, or hedging. Suppose that an economy is presently in a growth stage and a slowdown or recession is expected in the future. The desire to hedge will induce consumers to purchase financial instruments that deliver payoffs during economic slowdowns. A typical instrument of this type would be a long-term bond. As the demand for long-term bonds increases, the prices of the bonds rise in parallel, reducing the yields to maturity. Consumers will sell their short-term assets to finance their bond purchases. The pressure to sell these short-term instruments drives down their prices and consequently raises their yields. This is why we see falling long rates and rising short rates when a recession is expected. Under this condition, the term structure or yield curve (the difference between long-term and short-term rates) either flattens out or inverts. Thus, the yield spread provides a forecast of future economic growth. The yield spread has been described as one of the most useful indicators of economic activity.

Harvey (1989), among others, demonstrates the utility of the yield spread by measuring the relevance of data on US stock and bond markets for the forecasting of real economic activity. Harvey finds that stock market data and bond market data both contain information relevant for predicting economic growth, but that the latter delivers more accurate predictions. Yield curve measures explain more than 30 percent of the variation in economic growth over the period from 1953 to 1989, while the stock market variables explain only about five percent. Forecasts based on the yield curve compare favorably with forecasts from leading econometric models, whereas forecasts from stock market models do not. In a similar analysis extended to G7 countries, Harvey (1991) finds that the yield spread forecasts account for a large portion of the actual variation in the real economic growth of the G7 countries. A similar study by Estrella and Hardouvelis (1991) demonstrates that the yield spread in the United States contains information on the probability of a recession in that economy, as well as future growth in output, consumption, and investment.

Since the publication of Harvey's excellent findings in 1989, many researchers have analyzed whether the yield spread provides additional information for predicting future economic growth when other explanatory variables are included in the model. Haubrich and Dombrosky (1996) and Hamilton and Kim (2002), for example, extend Harvey's model to include the lagged economic growth rate as an additional explanatory variable. These authors note that the yield spread still provides additional information beyond that contained in the lagged growth rates. They also demonstrate that the statistical significance of the estimated coefficient on the spread conforms to a pattern similar to that found in models without the lagged economic growth rates as explanatory variables.

Other investigators analyze whether they can alter the relevance of the yield spread for predicting future economic activities by including variables to proxy monetary policy. In analyses by Estrella and Hardouvelis (1991), Plosser and Rouwenhorst (1994), Estrella and Mishkin (1997), and Hamilton and Kim (2002), for example, the yield spread still offers additional information beyond that contained in monetary policy variables.

Hamilton and Kim (2002) analyze whether the yield spread contains additional information on future economic activity, over and above the information contained in oil prices and oil price changes. This is conceptually similar to the work from Hamilton (1983). The underlying rationale holds that oil is a major determinant of the macroeconomic activities of industrialized countries. The coefficient on the yield spread remains statistically significant in their results. Galbraith and Tkacz (2000), on the other hand, search for possible asymmetries in the relationship between the yield spread-output links. To analyze whether the yield spread has an asymmetric impact on the conditional expectations of output growth, they test for a threshold effect in the relation. They find, as a result, that changes in the spread between long-term and short-term interest rates accurately predict changes in the outputs of G7 countries except Japan.

Taken together, these investigations suggest that the yield spread can be recognized as a well-established and leading indicator for future economic activity. This chapter sheds new light on this relationship by considering the influence of the US yield spread in an analysis of the relationship between the yield spread and future economic growth in the euro area. Most analyses on this issue have focused on the relationship between economic activity and the domestic yield spread. Newer studies, however, have explored the notion of a global transmission of interest rates. Frankel, Schmukler, and Servén (2004) provide evidence of a full transmission of international interest rates using a large sample comprising both developing and developed countries. Their results hold true even when exchange rates are fully floating. This, coupled with the predominance of the US as the world's largest economy, suggests that the yield spread in the US might have explanatory power for growth rates in other economies. Bhar and Hamori (2007), meanwhile, find that the US yield spread and domestic yield spread in Japan both help to explain future domestic economic growth in Japan within the framework of a Markov switching model.

We use two types of models to analyze the relationship between yield spread and future output growth in the euro area. Model 1 analyzes the relationship between economic growth and the domestic yield spread. Model 2 considers the respective roles of the US yield spread and domestic yield spread in explaining future economic growth in the euro area. We also empirically analyze these models in the euro area using both aggregate and panel data. Lacking aggregate data of a sufficient size on the euro area, we make a meaningful improvement by increasing the power of the statistical tests using panel data.

6.2.   Models

Harvey (1988) analyzes the planning problem for a representative consumer under the assumption of constant relative risk aversion (CRRA). This leads, under certain technical assumptions, to a simple empirical specification that connects the yield spread and the output growth in the economy. Investigations of this empirical specification have been reported by Harvey (1989, 1991), and later by Hamilton and Kim (2002), amongst others. Here we apply the model below, following the example of Hamilton and Kim (2002):

$$\text{Model 1: } y_t^k = \beta_0 + \beta_1 Spread_t + u_t, \tag{6.1}$$

where $y_t^k (= (1200/k)(\ln(\Upsilon_{t+k}) - \ln(\Upsilon_t)))$ is the annualized output growth rate over the next k periods, Υ_t is the real output at time t, $Spread_t (= R_t^{LR} - R_t^{SR})$ is the yield spread at time t, R_t^{LR} is the long-term interest rate at time t, R_t^{SR} is the short-term interest rate at time t, u_t is a stationary error term at time t, and β_0 and β_1 are constants. Note that the coefficient β_1 represents the average level of risk tolerance in the economy. Thus, $1/\beta_1$ is the average level of risk aversion.

Next, the model is extended to include the influence of the US yield spread on the euro area:

$$\text{Model 2 : } y_t^k = \beta_0 + \beta_1 Spread_t + \beta_2 Spread_t^{US} + \varepsilon_t, \tag{6.2}$$

where $Spread_t^{US}$ is the yield spread in the United States at time t and ε_t is a stationary error term. Equation (6.2) shows that the economic growth rate depends on the US yield spread, in addition to the domestic yield spread. If the US yield spread affects the economic growth of the euro area, the β_2 coefficient will be statistically significant.

As the data overlap in equations (6.1) and (6.2), the residuals inevitably have autocorrelation. To adjust for this problem, we obtain the adjusted t-statistics using the technique of Newey and West (1987).

6.3.   Aggregate Data Analysis

6.3.1.   *Data*

We perform our empirical analysis using monthly data covering the sample period between January 1999 and December 2007. The data are taken from the *International Financial Statistics* (International Monetary Fund). The analyses in this chapter use the short-term interest rate, long-term interest rate, and seasonally adjusted industrial production index. The yield spread offers an advantage over the changes in the short-term rate alone. Specifically, it serves as a better indicator of deliberate policy actions, insofar as the effects of real shocks can be dampened (Galbraith and Tkacz, 2000). Figure 6.1 shows the movements of yield spread and annualized output growth rate over the

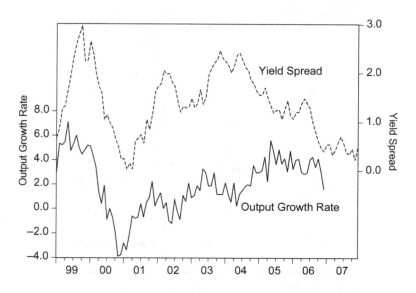

Fig. 6.1.   Yield Spread and Output Growth.

next 12 months. The yield spread and output growth over the sample period seems to be closely associated with each other.

6.3.2. *Empirical Results*

Table 6.1 shows the empirical results of equation (6.1) by the ordinary least squares (OLS) method. The estimated slope parameter (β_1) tends to get smaller as k gets bigger, as the following values illustrate: 1.520 ($k=2$), 1.602 ($k=3$), 1.474 ($k=4$), 1.354 ($k=6$), 1.424 ($k=9$), 1.373 ($k=12$), 1.032 ($k=18$), and 0.886 ($k=24$). The slope parameter (β_1) is not statistically significant at the five percent level for relatively short horizons (i.e., $k=2, 3, 4, 6$, and 9), but it is statistically significant at the five percent level for relatively long horizons (i.e., $k=12, 18$, and 24). These estimates are qualitatively similar to those

Table 6.1. Predicting Future Output Growth Based on the Yield Spread.

Model 2: $y_t^k = \beta_0 + \beta_1 Spread_t + u_t$

k (months ahead)	$\hat{\beta}_0$	$\hat{\beta}_1$	$\bar{R}^2$
2	−0.006	1.520	0.031
	(1.532)	(0.878)	
3	−0.091	1.602	0.074
	(1.517)	(0.869)	
4	0.079	1.474	0.069
	(1.489)	(0.852)	
6	0.255	1.354	0.091
	(1.486)	(0.853)	
9	0.049	1.424	0.131
	(1.307)	(0.760)	
12	0.001	1.373*	0.143
	(1.126)	(0.642)	
18	0.312	1.032*	0.112
	(0.900)	(0.459)	
24	0.344	0.886*	0.128
	(0.816)	(0.423)	

Note: Numbers in parentheses are standard error.
*denotes significance at the five percent level.

obtained by Hamilton and Kim (2002). The current analysis likewise concludes that the spread may contain information useful for the predictability of future economic activity in the euro area. We also see from Table 6.1 that $\bar{R}^2$ takes its highest value at $k = 12$.

Table 6.2 shows the empirical results for equation (6.2). This model considers the effect of not only the domestic yield spread of the euro area, but also the yield spread of the US. The parameter β_1 indicates the effect of the domestic yield spread on domestic output growth, while β_2 indicates the effect of the US yield spread on domestic output growth.

The estimated slope parameter (β_1) tends to get smaller as k becomes larger, as the following values show: 3.604 ($k = 2$), 3.715 ($k = 3$), 3.490 ($k = 4$), 3.205 ($k = 6$), 2.913 ($k = 9$), 2.467 ($k = 12$),

Table 6.2. Predicting Future Output Growth Based on the Domestic and US Yield Spreads.

Model 2: $y_t^k = \beta_0 + \beta_1 Spread_t + \beta_2 Spread_t^{US} + \varepsilon_t$

k (months ahead)	$\hat{\beta}_0$	$\hat{\beta}_1$	$\hat{\beta}_2$	$\bar{R}^2$
2	−0.304	3.604**	−1.767**	0.140
	(1.161)	(0.787)	(0.354)	
3	−0.405	3.715**	−1.786**	0.293
	(1.162)	(0.838)	(0.356)	
4	−0.239	3.490**	−1.695**	0.294
	(1.165)	(0.766)	(0.337)	
6	−0.024	3.205**	−1.562**	0.394
	(1.198)	(0.717)	(0.304)	
9	−0.117	2.913**	−1.284**	0.402
	(1.154)	(0.589)	(0.251)	
12	−0.028	2.467**	−0.989**	0.337
	(1.093)	(0.459)	(0.269)	
18	0.412	1.532**	−0.501	0.179
	(0.953)	(0.470)	(0.313)	
24	0.352	0.907	−0.023	0.118
	(0.862)	(0.469)	(0.270)	

Note: Numbers in parentheses are standard error.
**denotes significance at the one percent level.

1.532 ($k = 18$), and 0.907 ($k = 24$). Note that when the US effect is considered, β_1 is statistically significant at the one percent level for both relatively short horizons (i.e., $k = 2, 3, 4, 6$, and 9) and relatively long horizons (i.e., $k = 12$ and 18). The absolute value of the estimated β_2 coefficient tends to get smaller as k gets bigger, as follows: -1.767 ($k = 2$), -1.786 ($k = 3$), -1.695 ($k = 4$), -1.562 ($k = 6$), -1.284 ($k = 9$), -0.989 ($k = 12$), -0.501 ($k = 18$) and -0.023 ($k = 24$). Here, the estimated parameter is statistically significant at the one percent level for $k = 2, 3, 4, 6, 9$, and 12. Thus, the domestic yield spread and the US yield spread are both significant explanatory variables for domestic economic growth in the euro area. The estimates for β_1 are clearly biased downward if we ignore the effects of the US yield spread on the future growth of domestic output in the euro area. We also see from Table 6.2 that $\bar{R}^2$ takes its highest value at $k = 9$.

The results of the CUSUM of squares tests for model 1 and model 2 for $k = 12$ are shown in Figures 6.2 and 6.3, respectively. The

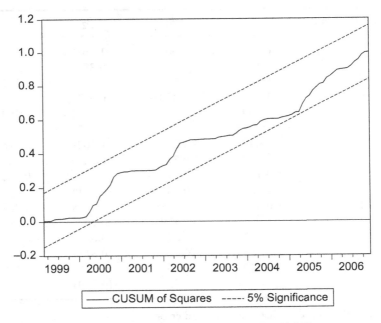

Fig. 6.2.   CUSUM of Square Tests (Model 1).

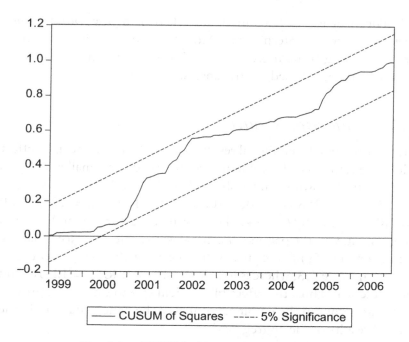

Fig. 6.3. CUSUM of Square Tests (Model 2).

CUSUM of squares test is often used to test for structural stability. This provides a plot of the test statistic and a pair of five percent critical lines. The movements outside the critical lines suggest that there may be structural change during the sample period. As clearly seen in the figures, both models seem to remain stable during the sample period.

6.4. Panel Data Analysis

6.4.1. *Data*

Next, we carry out a similar analysis with monthly panel data of 11 countries in the euro area: Austria, Belgium, Finland, France, Germany, Ireland, Italy, Luxembourg, Netherlands, Portugal, and Spain. The sample period extends from January 1999 to December

2007. The data for each country are taken from the *International Financial Statistics* (International Monetary Fund). The short-term interest rate, long-term interest rate, and seasonally adjusted industrial production index are used for the analysis.

6.4.2. *Empirical Results*

Table 6.3 presents the empirical results of model 1 using the fixed effect model. The estimated slope parameter (β_1) tends get smaller as k gets bigger, as the following values show: 1.557 $(k = 2)$, 1.574 $(k = 3)$, 1.476 $(k = 4)$, 1.288 $(k = 6)$, 1.405 $(k = 9)$, 1.200 $(k = 12)$, 0.730 $(k = 18)$, and 0.536 $(k = 24)$. The parameter estimates of Table 6.3 are consistent with the parameter estimates of Table 6.1. Note that the slope parameter (β_1) is statistically significant at the five percent level for $k > 2$ in Table 6.3, whereas it is significant only for $k = 12, 18$, and 24 in Table 6.1. Thus, the effect of the yield spread on output growth is more significant in the empirical results of the panel data than in the empirical results of the aggregate data.

Table 6.3. Predicting Future Output Growth Based on the Yield Spread Panel Data Analysis: Fixed Effect Model.

Model 1: $y_{it}^k = \beta_{0i} + \beta_1 Spread_{it} + u_{it}$

k (months ahead)	$\hat{\beta}_1$	$\bar{R}^2$
2	1.557 (1.041)	0.005
3	1.574* (0.746)	0.020
4	1.476* (0.688)	0.033
6	1.288** (0.501)	0.068
9	1.405** (0.464)	0.114
12	1.200** (0.374)	0.161
18	0.730** (0.274)	0.241
24	0.536* (0.225)	0.306

Note: Numbers in parentheses are standard error.
*denotes significance at the five percent level.
**denotes significance at the one percent level.

Table 6.4. Predicting Future Output Growth Based on the Yield Spread Panel Data Analysis: Random Effect Model.

Model 1: $y_{it}^k = \beta_0 + \beta_1 Spread_{it} + u_{it}$

k (months ahead)	$\hat{\beta}_1$	$\bar{R}^2$
2	1.461* (0.734)	0.003
3	1.529** (0.528)	0.007
4	1.447** (0.428)	0.009
6	1.274** (0.311)	0.014
9	1.396** (0.240)	0.029
12	1.195** (0.202)	0.031
18	0.728** (0.154)	0.021
24	0.534** (0.126)	0.018

Note: Numbers in parentheses are standard error.
*denotes significance at the five percent level.
**denotes significance at the one percent level.

Table 6.4 presents the empirical results of model 1 based on the random effect model.[1] The estimated slope parameter (β_1) here also tends to get smaller as k gets bigger, as the following values show: 1.461 ($k = 2$), 1.529 ($k = 3$), 1.447 ($k = 4$), 1.274 ($k = 6$), 1.396 ($k = 9$), 1.195 ($k = 12$), 0.728 ($k = 18$), and 0.534 ($k = 24$). The parameter estimates of the random effect model (Table 6.4) are consistent with the parameter estimates of the fixed effect model (Table 6.3). Note that the slope parameter (β_1) is statistically significant at the five percent level for $k > 1$. As found earlier with the fixed effect model, the effect of the yield spread on output growth is more significant in the empirical results based on the random effect model than in the empirical results of the aggregate data.

Table 6.5 shows the empirical results of model 2 based on the fixed effect model. This model considers the effects of both the domestic

---

[1] This fixed effect model is an appropriate specification if we focus on a specific set of N individuals and our inference is restricted to the behavior of these sets of individuals. By contrast, the random effect model is an appropriate specification if we are drawing N individuals randomly from a large population. (See Baltagi, 2005).

Table 6.5. Predicting Future Output Growth Based on the Domestic and US Yield Spreads Panel Data Analysis: Fixed Effect Model.

Model 2: $y_{it}^k = \beta_{0i} + \beta_1 Spread_{it} + \beta_2 Spread_t^{US} + \varepsilon_{it}$

k (months ahead)	$\hat{\beta}_1$	$\hat{\beta}_2$	$\bar{R}^2$
2	3.205**	−1.447**	0.011
	(0.927)	(0.497)	
3	3.209**	−1.434**	0.034
	(0.649)	(0.346)	
4	3.025**	−1.352**	0.051
	(0.533)	(0.282)	
6	2.585**	−1.138**	0.093
	(0.383)	(0.200)	
9	2.505**	−0.989**	0.147
	(0.289)	(0.151)	
12	2.008**	−0.764**	0.189
	(0.238)	(0.124)	
18	1.162**	−0.457**	0.259
	(0.176)	(0.093)	
24	0.668**	−0.148	0.307
	(0.145)	(0.080)	

Note: Numbers in parentheses are standard error.
**denotes significance at the one percent level.

yield spread and the US yield spread. The parameters β_1 and β_2 represent the respective effects of the domestic yield spread and the US yield spread on domestic output growth.

The estimated slope parameter β_1 tends to get smaller as k gets bigger, as the following values show: 3.205 ($k = 2$), 3.209 ($k = 3$), 3.025 ($k = 4$), 2.585 ($k = 6$), 2.505 ($k = 9$), 2.008 ($k = 12$), 1.162 ($k = 18$), and 0.668 ($k = 24$). Note that β_1 is statistically significant at the five percent level for every k. Likewise, the absolute value of the estimated β_2 coefficient tends to get smaller as k gets bigger, as follows: −1.447 ($k = 2$), −1.434 ($k = 3$), −1.352 ($k = 4$), −1.138 ($k = 6$), −0.989 ($k = 9$), −0.764 ($k = 12$), −0.457 ($k = 18$), and

-0.148 ($k = 24$). Here, the estimated β_2 is statistically significant at the one percent level for most cases. Thus, the domestic yield spread and the US yield spread are both significant explanatory variables for future output growth in the euro area. Here, again, the estimates for β_1 are biased downward if we ignore the effects of US yield spread on domestic future output growth in the euro area. These results in Table 6.5 are basically consistent with the results in Table 6.2.

Table 6.6 shows the empirical results of model 2 based the random effect model. Here, the estimated slope parameter β_1 tends to get smaller as k gets bigger, as the following values show: 3.032 ($k = 2$), 3.129 ($k = 3$), 2.973 ($k = 4$), 2.561 ($k = 6$), 2.491 ($k = 9$), 2.000 ($k = 12$), 1.158 ($k = 18$), and 0.666 ($k = 24$). Note that β_1 is

Table 6.6. Predicting Future Output Growth Based on the Domestic and US Yield Spreads Panel Data Analysis: Random Effect Model.

Model 2: $y_{it}^k = \beta_0 + \beta_1 Spread_{it} + \beta_2 Spread_t^{US} + \varepsilon_{it}$

k (months ahead)	$\hat{\beta}_1$	$\hat{\beta}_2$	$\bar{R}^2$
2	3.032**	−1.390**	0.008
	(0.922)	(0.496)	
3	3.129**	−1.408**	0.020
	(0.648)	(0.346)	
4	2.973**	−1.335**	0.027
	(0.532)	(0.282)	
6	2.561**	−1.131**	0.040
	(0.382)	(0.200)	
9	2.491**	−0.985**	0.065
	(0.289)	(0.151)	
12	2.000**	−0.762**	0.064
	(0.237)	(0.124)	
18	1.158**	−0.456**	0.043
	(0.176)	(0.093)	
24	0.666**	−0.148	0.021
	(0.145)	(0.080)	

Note: Numbers in parentheses are standard error.
**denotes significance at the one percent level.

statistically significant at the one percent level for every case. Likewise, the absolute value of the estimated β_2 coefficient also tends to get smaller as k gets bigger, as follows: -1.390 ($k = 2$), -1.408 ($k = 3$), -1.335 ($k = 4$), -1.131 ($k = 6$), -0.985 ($k = 9$), -0.762 ($k = 12$), -0.456 ($k = 18$), and -0.148 ($k = 24$). Here, the estimated β_2 is statistically significant at the one percent level for most cases. Thus, the domestic yield spread and the US yield spread are both significant explanatory variables for future output growth in the euro area. These results in Table 6.6 are basically consistent with the results in Table 6.5.

6.5.   Some Concluding Remarks

To derive the most benefit from an economic indicator, the indicator should be measured in a precise and timely fashion. The yield spread is amenable to this type of measurement. It can be observed immediately and with virtually no measurement error. This distinguishes it from many other macroeconomic data series.

This chapter empirically analyzes the relationship between the yield spread and the future output growth rate based on aggregate and panel data in the euro area from January 1999 to December 2007. The main empirical results can be summarized as follows:

(1) In an analysis of the effect of the domestic yield spread on future output growth based on aggregate data, the yield spread serves as a significant explanatory variable for future economic growth over a relatively long time horizon, such as one or two years.

(2) When the US yield spread is included as an additional explanatory variable, the domestic and US yield spreads are both significant explanatory variables for future output growth over most time horizons. This provides some empirical evidence to support the influence of the US economy on the euro area.

(3) In an analysis of the effect of the domestic yield spread on future output growth based on panel data, the yield spread serves as a significant explanatory variable for output growth over most time horizons.

(4) When the US yield spread is included as an additional explanatory variable, both yield spreads significantly explain the movements of future output growth over most time horizons. This provides more empirical evidence that the US economy influences the economies of the euro area.

(5) The estimates for the coefficient of the average risk tolerance are biased downward if we ignore the effects of the US yield spread on the future growth of domestic output in the euro area.

International Capital Flows
and the Feldstein–Horioka Paradox

7.1. Introduction

Since the seminal work of Feldstein and Horioka (1980), the measurement of the freedom of international capital flows has been a research theme of great interest to many researchers in the field of international economics.

In an absence of international capital flows, borrowing from abroad cannot compensate for shortages in domestic saving. As a consequence, shortages in domestic saving lead to shortages in domestic investment. Conversely, when domestic saving increases, all of the increased saving is directed to domestic investment. Thus, domestic saving and domestic investment are strongly correlated in a closed economy.

In an economy with capital flowing freely in and out of a country, borrowing from abroad can compensate for shortages in domestic saving. Declines in domestic saving, therefore, do not necessarily lead to declines in domestic investment. From the opposite perspective, increases in domestic saving do not necessarily flow into domestic investment. In many cases, the savings may be directed abroad in search of higher investment returns. Thus, domestic saving and domestic investment are not strongly correlated in an open economy.

To empirically test the above relationship between saving and investment rates, Feldstein and Horioka (1980) apply the following equation:

$$\frac{I}{Y} = \alpha + \beta\left(\frac{S}{Y}\right) \qquad (7.1)$$

where I/Y is the investment rate and S/Y is the saving rate. If international capital flows are completely unrestricted, the saving rate coefficient, β, approaches zero. If, on the other hand, there are no international capital flows, nearly all increases in saving are used for domestic investment and β approaches one.

Feldstein and Horioka (1980) obtain β estimates of close to one in an analysis of the relationship between saving and investment rates using data from 16 industrialized countries (Australia, Austria, Belgium, Canada, Denmark, Finland, Germany, Greece, Ireland, Italy, Japan, the Netherlands, New Zealand, Sweden, the United Kingdom, and the United States) from 1960 to 1974. This result is called the "Feldstein–Horioka puzzle", as it clearly refutes the hypothesis that capital flows are unrestricted. The research by Feldstein and Horioka (1980) has been examined with great interest by many researchers. Subsequent analyses suggest that results similar to those of Feldstein and Horioka (1980) can be obtained for the OECD countries (Feldstein, 1983; Murphy, 1984; Obstfeld, 1986; Golub, 1990; Feldstein and Bacchetta, 1991; Tesar, 1991; Obstfeld, 1995).

In an analysis of the disparity of the saving-investment correlation, Frankel *et al.* (1986) clearly demonstrate that saving rate coefficients are larger in industrialized countries than in developing countries. When this finding is published, it overturns the common wisdom. By the earlier reasoning, a relatively high level of regulation in a developing country reflects relatively strong constraints on inward and outward capital flows. This implies, in turn, that domestic saving and investment are strongly linked, and that the saving rate coefficient should be large in developing countries. The results from Frankel *et al.* (1986) directly contradict these assumptions. These are important findings and raise the critical question of why the saving rate coefficients of developing countries are small. Hamori (2007) refers to this question as the "Frankel–Dooley–Mathieson puzzle".

Experiments with many analytical devices have been applied in attempts to resolve the Feldstein–Horioka puzzle. Here we will describe three. The first device (Obstfeld, 1986; Artis and Bayoumi, 1989) is to consider other elements as additional explanatory variables to lower the regression coefficient for domestic savings, such as fiscal variables, shocks to domestic investment and domestic savings, and the effect of non-traded commodities. The second device (Bayoumi and Rose, 1993; Dekle, 1996) is to examine cross-section data for various regions of a country to test the assertions of Feldstein and Horioka (1980). The third device (Coiteux and Olivier, 2000; Ho, 2002) is to test the results of Feldstein and Horioka (1980) with explicit consideration of the non-stationarity of data.

This chapter empirically analyzes the savings-and-investment relationship in the euro area using panel data over the period between 1980 and 2005. Specifically, we conduct a non-stationary panel time series analysis. Non-stationary time series analyses of unit roots, co-integration, etc. lose accuracy when the sample sizes are small. We cope with this issue here by applying panel co-integration methods to determine the robustness of empirical results. We also conduct a sub-sample analysis to explore effects of the capital market integration in the euro area.

7.2. Data

Figure 7.1 indicates the movements of saving and investment rates for the aggregate 11 countries of the euro area: Austria, Belgium, Finland, France, Germany, Ireland, Italy, Luxembourg, the Netherlands, Portugal, and Spain. As the figure shows, investment rate and saving rate tend to move together between 1980 and the middle of the 1990s, but then start to deviate.[1]

For empirical analysis, we use the panel data of these 11 countries over the period from 1980 to 2005 (annual data). Data on saving and investment rates are included. The saving rate for each country is the gross domestic savings as a percentage of GDP. The investment rate of each country is the gross capital formation as a percentage of GDP.

---

[1]The saving rate is calculated as the sum of the gross domestic savings (measured in current US dollars) of the countries divided by the sum of the GDPs (measured in current US dollars). The investment rate is calculated as the sum of gross capital formation (measured in current US dollars) divided by the sum of the GDPs (measured in current US dollars). The data are taken from the World Development Indicators (World Development Bank).

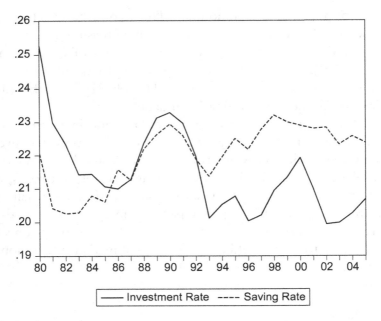

Fig. 7.1.   Investment Rate and Saving Rate in the Euro Area.

The data are taken from the World Development Indicators (The World Bank).

As a preliminary analysis, we check whether or not the saving and investment rates have unit roots. According to the panel unit root test developed by Levin *et al.* (2003), we find that the null hypothesis of a unit root is likely to be accepted for the level of each variable and is clearly rejected for the first difference of each variable. Thus, each variable may be a I(1) variable with a unit root.

7.3.   Empirical Model

Next, we use the following model to test the results reported by Feldstein and Horioka (1980).

$$\left(\frac{I}{Y}\right)_{i,t} = \alpha_i + \beta \left(\frac{S}{Y}\right)_{i,t} + u_{i,t}, \quad i = 1, 2, \ldots, N, \quad t = 1, 2, \ldots, T$$

$$(7.2)$$

where I represents domestic investment; S, domestic saving; Y, GDP; T, the number of observations over time; and N, the number of individual members in the panel.

If international capital flows are completely unrestricted, the saving rate coefficient, β, should approach zero. This implies that there is no co-integrating relationship between saving and investment rates. If, on the other hand, there are no international capital flows, nearly all increases in saving will be used for domestic investment, and β will approach one. This implies that there is a co-integrating relationship between saving and investment rates with a co-integrating vector of $\beta = 1$.

7.4. Empirical Results

Having found that each of the saving and investment rates has a unit root, we can carry out the co-integration analysis for equation (7.2). For this, we rely on the Pedroni-type panel co-integration tests developed by Pedroni (1999, 2001). Table 7.1 shows the results. Here we investigate four statistics, i.e., the Panel PP (Phillips and Perron) test, Panel ADF (augmented Dickey–Fuller) test, Group PP test, and Group ADF test. The null hypothesis is no co-integrating relation, and the alternative hypothesis is the existence of a co-integrating relation. For the Panel PP and Panel ADF tests, the alternative hypothesis assumes that there is a homogeneous AR coefficient among countries. For the Group PP and Group ADF tests, the alternative hypothesis recognizes heterogeneous AR coefficients among countries. Under the null hypothesis of no co-integration, the test statistic and its p-value are -2.267 and 0.012 for the Panel PP test, -2.303 and 0.011 for the Panel ADF test, -1.705 and 0.044 for the Group PP test, and -3.200 and 0.001 for the Group ADF test. Thus, the null hypothesis of no co-integration is rejected in all cases at the five percent significance level.

Next, we conduct the Johansen-type panel co-integration tests developed by Maddala and Wu (1999).[2] Fisher (1932) derives a

---

[2]See Johansen (1991) and Johansen and Juselius (1990).

Table 7.1.　Panel Co-integration Tests.
Pedroni Tests (1980–2005)

	Test statistics	p-value
Panel PP test	−2.267	0.012
Panel ADF test	−2.303	0.011
Group PP test	−1.705	0.044
Group ADF test	−3.200	0.001

combined test based on results of the individual independent tests. Maddala and Wu (1999) draw from Fisher's result to propose an approach to testing for co-integration in panel data by combining tests from individual cross-sections into a test statistic for the full panel. Two kinds of Johansen-type test have been developed: The Fisher test from the trace test, and the Fisher test from the maximum eigenvalue test. In the Johansen-type panel co-integration test, the empirical results depend heavily on the VAR system lag order. Here we confirm the robustness of our empirical results by indicating the results when the lag order is first and when the lag order is second. If p_i is the p-value from an individual co-integration test for cross-section i, then under the null hypothesis for the panel, $-2 \sum_{i=1}^{N} \log(p_i)$ has an asymptotic chi-square distribution with degrees of freedom equal to $2N$, where N is the number of cross-sections. Table 7.2 shows the results.

Under the null hypothesis of no co-integration, the Fisher statistics from the trace test and maximum eigenvalue test are 65.320 and 54.150 respectively, with a p-value of 0.000 in each case, when the lag length is equal to one. When the lag length is equal to two, the Fisher statistics from the trace test and maximum eigenvalue test are 83.980 and 72.110, respectively, with a p-value of 0.000 in each case. Thus, the null hypothesis of no co-integration is rejected for every case at the one percent significance level.

Having confirmed a co-integrating relation between the saving and investment rates, we estimate the co-integrating vector by the panel dynamic ordinary least squares (panel DOLS) method

Table 7.2. Panel Co-integration Tests. Johansen-type Tests (1980–2005).

H_0	Fisher statistic from trace test	p-value	Fisher statistic from maximum eigenvalue test	p-value
Lag length is 1.				
$r = 0$	65.320	0.000	54.150	0.000
Lag length is 2.				
$r = 0$	83.980	0.000	72.110	0.000

Note: r is the number of co-integrating vectors.

Table 7.3. Panel Co-integrating Estimation: Panel DOLS.

K	β	t-value
2	0.297	8.252
3	0.245	5.013

Note: K is the number of leads and lags in dynamic OLS.

developed by Stock and Watson (1993) based on the following equation[3]:

$$\left(\frac{I}{Y}\right)_{i,t} = \alpha_i + \beta_i \left(\frac{S}{Y}\right)_{i,t} + \sum_{j=-K}^{K} \gamma_{ij} \Delta \left(\frac{S}{Y}\right)_{i,t-j} + v_{i,t}, \quad (7.3)$$

where Δ is a difference operator, i.e., $\Delta x_t = x_t - x_{t-1}$; K is the number of leads and lags in Dynamic OLS; and $v_{i,t}$ is a stationary error term.

To check the robustness of empirical results, we use the order of leads and lags as two and three. As Table 7.3 shows, the estimated

---

[3] For panel DOLS, see Appendix A.

coefficient is 0.297 for $K = 2$ and 0.245 for $K = 3$, which is statistically significant at the one percent level in both cases. Thus, we obtain a relatively small coefficient for the euro area over the sample period. This may indicate that a relatively small portion of the increase in saving is used for domestic investment in the euro area.

7.5. Sub-Sample Analysis

To examine the empirical results in more detail, we check the panel co-integration tests for sub-samples. First, we divide the whole sample into three sub-samples: 1980–1989, 1990–1999, and 2000–2005. Table 7.4 shows the results of Pedroni tests for each sub-sample period. At the 10 percent level of significance, the null hypothesis of no co-integration is rejected in three of four cases for 1980–1989, two of four cases for 1990–1999, and no cases for 2000–2005. Thus, the hull of no co-integration is not likely to be rejected as time passes. In other words, the stable relationship between saving and investment rates tends to disappear as capital markets become more integrated in the euro area.

Table 7.4.   Panel Co-integration Tests: Sub-Sample Analysis.

Sample period	Method	Test statistic	p-value
1980–1989	Panel PP test	−1.456	0.073
	Panel ADF test	−2.514	0.006
	Group PP test	−0.977	0.164
	Group ADF test	−1.463	0.072
1990–1999	Panel PP test	−0.845	0.199
	Panel ADF test	−2.384	0.009
	Group PP test	0.050	0.520
	Group ADF test	−1.639	0.051
2000–2005	Panel PP test	0.195	0.577
	Panel ADF test	0.391	0.652
	Group PP test	0.383	0.649
	Group ADF test	1.292	0.902

7.6. Some Concluding Remarks

This chapter analyzes the relationship between saving rates and investment rates based on panel data from 1980 through 2005 in the euro area. The empirical results leave us with two important findings.

(1) There is a co-integrating relation between saving and investment rates for the whole sample. The estimated coefficients of the saving rate are 0.297 and 0.245, values which are statistically significant. This may indicate that a relatively small portion of the increase in saving is used for domestic investment in the euro area.

(2) The co-integrating relation tends to be rejected for recent samples. This may indicate that the stable relationship between saving and investment rates tends to disappear as capital markets become more integrated in the euro area.

Nominal and Real Exchange Rate Fluctuations: Euro, US Dollar, and Japanese Yen

8.1. Introduction

An important step, in modeling exchange rates and studying economic policy, is to measure the relative importance of permanent and temporary shocks on exchange rates. Disequilibrium models of exchange rate determination (e.g., Dornbusch, 1976) mainly attribute variations in real and nominal exchange rates to nominal disturbances of types likely to have only transitory effects on real exchange rates. Equilibrium models (e.g., Stockman, 1987) rely on permanent, real shocks to explain movements in both real and nominal rates. Isolating these sources of variation can assist policymakers in determining the extent of excess variability in exchange rates (Lastrapes, 1992). A thorough understanding of the sources underlying real exchange rate fluctuations is also crucial, given that this rate reflects the performance and competitiveness of an economy. Movements in the real exchange rate may also influence inflation, output, and the balance of payments.

This chapter investigates the sources of real exchange rate fluctuations for the euro area, the United States, and Japan. By constructing a structural VAR (SVAR) model to analyze the sources of real exchange rate fluctuations, we try to identify the forces driving the fluctuations from 1999 to 2007.

Blanchard and Quah (1989) published an influential work based on a bivariate structural VAR model for output and unemployment. In the years since, several studies have attempted to investigate the sources driving real exchange rate fluctuations. Bayoumi and

Eichengreen (1992) and Lastrapes (1992) were among the first to analyze exchange rate variations using the Blanchard and Quah (1989) approach. Bayoumi and Eichengreen (1992) distinguish between supply shocks and demand shocks by assuming that the former have permanent effects whereas the latter have only temporary effects. Their empirical results, for the G-7 countries, indicate that the shift from the Bretton Woods system of pegged exchange rates to the post-Bretton Woods float can be explained by a modest increase in the cross-country dispersion of supply shocks. Lastrapes (1992) carries out a similar analysis for six industrialized countries from 1973 to 1989. He identifies two types of structural disturbance, nominal shocks and real shocks, with the restriction that the former has no long-run impact on the real exchange rate. His results indicate that real shocks account for the major part of both real and nominal exchange rate fluctuations for all six of the countries analyzed.

This type of research is further developed by Enders and Lee (1997), Chowdhury (2004), and Hamori and Hamori (2007). Enders and Lee (1997) decompose real and nominal exchange rate variance into the components induced by real and nominal factors from 1973 to 1992. They find that nominal shocks have a minor effect on the real and nominal bilateral exchange rates of the Canadian, Japanese, and German currencies against the US dollar. Chowdhury (2004) investigates sources of variation in the real and nominal US dollar exchange rates of selected emerging market economies by decomposing the exchange rate series into stochastic components induced by real and nominal factors. His analysis focuses on the dynamic effects and relative importance of real and nominal shocks in explaining the behavior of these exchange rates. Hamori and Hamori (2007) analyze the sources of real and nominal exchange rate variance for the euro-dollar rate. Specifically, they examine the robustness of the results by considering different combinations of data on nominal exchange rates and price indices. In doing so, they find that the shape of the impulse response function differs substantially from index to index.

Clarida and Gali (1994) extend the bivariate VAR model to the trivariate VAR model and identify three types of structural disturbance: real aggregate supply shocks (those capable of influencing the levels of all three variables in the long run), real aggregate demand shocks (those with no long-run impact on the real output level), and nominal shocks (those that affect only the price level in the long run). According to their empirical analysis for four industrialized countries (Germany, Japan, the UK, and Canada) over the floating period from 1973 to 1992, the variation in the real exchange rates against the dollar is mainly driven by nominal disturbances in two of the countries (Germany and Japan: 41 percent and 35 percent of the variance in the dollar-deutschmark and dollar-yen real exchange rates respectively), whereas the variations in the other two countries are mainly driven by real demand shocks. Hamori and Hamori (2008b) analyzed the sources of real and nominal exchange rate variance for the euro-dollar rate, applying the SVAR methods of Clarida and Gali (1994). Their empirical results indicate that real shocks are the dominant explanatory factors behind the real exchange rate fluctuations in the euro-dollar rate.

These studies set a benchmark for our explanations of real exchange rate variance in this chapter. We begin by constructing a bivariate structural vector autoregressive (SVAR) model consisting of real and nominal effective exchange rates. We assess the relative importance of two types of shocks: real shocks and nominal shocks. Next, we extend the model to a trivariate SVAR model consisting of output, real effective exchange rates, and nominal effective exchange rates. Here, we assess the relative importance of three types of shocks: real supply shocks, real demand shocks, and nominal shocks.

Though much of the existing literature relies on bilateral exchange rates, this chapter uses the effective exchange rates of the euro area (euro), the United States (dollar), and Japan (yen). The effective exchange rate reflects international competitiveness of a country. The competitiveness of a country cannot be understood simply by examining exchange rates between the home currency and the currencies of other countries. An analysis of the sources behind the variation in the real effective exchange rate helps us understand the international competitiveness of the country overall. We compare the relative importance of each shock in driving the movements in the real effective exchange rates of the euro, US dollar, and Japanese yen.

8.2.   Data

The data are taken from the *International Financial Statistics* (International Monetary Fund). Our empirical analysis in this chapter is based on monthly observations of the period between January 1999 and December 2007. We use the nominal effective exchange rate, real effective exchange rate, and industrial production index (seasonally adjusted) of the euro area, the United States, and Japan.

The nominal and real effective exchange rates are more meaningful for empirical analysis than bilateral exchange rates. The nominal effective exchange rate is the weighted average of a country's exchange rates against other major currencies. International competitiveness is affected not only by the exchange rate, but also by fluctuations in domestic and foreign prices. Thus, the nominal effective exchange rate is adjusted to incorporate inflation rate differences.[1] This type of indicator is called the real effective exchange rate.

The movements in the logs of real effective exchange rates for the euro, US dollar, and Japanese yen are respectively given in Figs. 8.1, 8.2, and 8.3. As the plots show, the real effective exchange rate of the euro appreciated sharply from 2000 to mid 2007, while those of the US dollar and Japanese yen fell sharply.

This chapter uses the augmented Dickey–Fuller (ADF) test (Dickey and Fuller, 1979) to test for the presence of a unit root for each variable in the univariate representations of the log of the nominal effective exchange rate (e_t), the log of the real effective exchange rate (r_t), and the log of the industrial production index (y_t). The null hypothesis of a unit root is not rejected at conventional significance levels for any of the variables for any country. The null hypothesis is rejected, however, for the first-difference of each variable for each country. Thus, e_t, r_t and y_t are all found to be I(1) series for all countries.

---

[1] For example, even if the nominal effective exchange rate of the euro remains unchanged, the relative competitiveness of goods in the euro area increases when the inflation rate of its trading partner is higher.

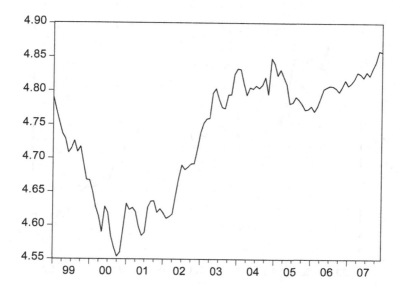

Fig. 8.1.   Log of the Real Effective Exchange Rate (Euro).

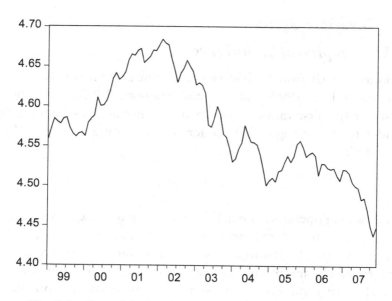

Fig. 8.2.   Log of the Real Effective Exchange Rate (US Dollar).

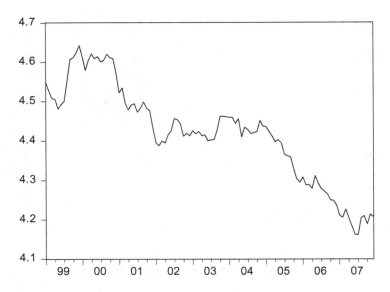

Fig. 8.3.   Log of the Real Effective Exchange Rate (Japanese Yen).

8.3.   Bivariate System

8.3.1.   *Empirical Techniques*

The bivariate VAR model will serve as a starting point for our discussion (Enders and Lee, 1997; Hamori and Hamori, 2007). This model consists of the first difference of real and nominal exchange rates. Consider the following infinite-order vector moving average (VMA) representation:

$$\Delta x_t = C(L)\varepsilon_t, \tag{8.1}$$

where L is a lag operator, Δ is a difference operator, $\Delta x_t = [\Delta r_t, \Delta e_t]'$ is a (2×1) vector of endogenous variables, and $\varepsilon_t = [\varepsilon_{r,t}, \varepsilon_{n,t}]'$ is a (2×1) vector of structural shocks with covariance matrix Σ. The error term can be interpreted as real shocks $(\varepsilon_{r,t})$ and nominal shocks $(\varepsilon_{n,t})$. The structural shocks are assumed to have no contemporaneous correlation or autocorrelation. This implies that Σ is a diagonal matrix.

To implement the econometric methodology, we need to estimate the following finite-order VAR model:

$$[I - \Phi(L)]\Delta x_t = u_t, \tag{8.2}$$

where $\Phi(L)$ is a finite-order matrix polynomial in the lag operator and u_t is a vector of disturbances. If the stationarity condition is satisfied, we can transfer equation (8.2) to the VMA representation:

$$\Delta x_t = A(L)u_t, \tag{8.3}$$

where $A(L)$ is a lag polynomial.

Equations (8.1) and (8.3) imply a linear relationship between ε_t and u_t:

$$u_t = C_0 \varepsilon_t. \tag{8.4}$$

C_0 in equation (8.4) is a 2×2 matrix defining a contemporaneous structural relationship to be identified for the vector of structural shocks ε_t in order to recover that vector from the estimated disturbance vector u_t. We need four parameters to convert the residuals from the estimated VAR into the original shocks driving the behavior of the endogenous variables. Three of the four are given by the elements of $\Sigma = C_0 C_0'$, hence we need to add one more identifying restriction. Blanchard and Quah (1989) propose the use of economic theory to impose this restriction. Following the methods of Enders and Lee (1997) and Hamori and Hamori (2007), we impose an additional restriction on the long-run multipliers while freely determining the short run dynamics. This restriction is written as follows:

Nominal (monetary) shocks have no long-run impact on the real exchange rate.

The long-run representation of equation (8.1) can be written as:

$$\begin{bmatrix} \Delta r_t \\ \Delta e_t \end{bmatrix} = \begin{bmatrix} C_{11}(1) & C_{12}(1) \\ C_{21}(1) & C_{22}(1) \end{bmatrix} \begin{bmatrix} \varepsilon_{r,t} \\ \varepsilon_{n,t} \end{bmatrix}, \tag{8.5}$$

where $C(1) = C_0 + C_1 + C_2 + \cdots$ are long-run multipliers of the structural VAR (long-run effect of ε_t on Δx_t). Assumption 8.1 implies that the long-run multiplier C_{12} is equal to zero, thus making $C(1)$ a lower triangular matrix.

The analysis in this chapter differs from the analyses from the existing paper such as Enders and Lee (1997) and Hamori and Hamori (2007). This chapter employs effective exchange rates, while Enders and Lee (1997) and Hamori and Hamori (2007) use bilateral exchange rates.

8.3.2. *Empirical Results*

When the SBIC (Schwarz Bayesian Information Criterion) is used to select the optimal lag length of VAR in empirical analysis, the VAR(1) model turns out to be the most appropriate for the euro, US dollar, and Japanese yen. To elucidate the sources behind the real exchange rate fluctuations, we carry out the forecast error variance decompositions. Variance decomposition is a useful technique for evaluating the relative importance of such shocks to the system.

Table 8.1 shows the fraction of the forecast error variance attributable to each shock at different time horizons in the bivariate model for the euro. Real shocks account for more than 99 percent of the variance in the real effective exchange rate throughout the estimation horizons. Less than one percent of variance remaining is attributable to nominal shocks. The estimates imply that real shocks explain most of the variance in the real effective exchange rate.

In the forecast error variance decompositions for the variation in the nominal exchange rate, real shocks also explain most of the movement in the nominal exchange rate. Real shocks account for more than 99 percent of the variance in the nominal effective exchange rate. Nominal shocks, meanwhile, contribute less than one percent.

Table 8.2 shows the fraction of the forecast error variance attributable to each shock at different horizons in the bivariate model for each variable for the US dollar. Real shocks account for more than 97 percent of the variance in the real effective exchange rate throughout the estimation horizons. Nominal shocks, meanwhile, account for less

Table 8.1. Forecast Error Variance Decomposition with the Bivariate System: Euro.

Horizon (months)	Real shock (%)	Nominal shock (%)
(*a*) *Real Effective Exchange Rate*		
3	99.583	0.417
6	99.583	0.417
9	99.583	0.417
12	99.583	0.417
18	99.583	0.417
24	99.583	0.417
36	99.583	0.417
(*b*) *Nominal Effective Exchange Rate*		
3	99.811	0.189
6	99.811	0.190
9	99.811	0.190
12	99.811	0.190
18	99.811	0.190
24	99.811	0.190
36	99.811	0.190

than three percent. The estimates imply that real shocks explain most of the variance in the real effective exchange rate.

According to forecast error variance decompositions, real shocks explain most of the movement in the nominal effective exchange rate, as well. Real shocks account for more than 90 percent of the variance in the nominal effective exchange rate. Nominal shocks, meanwhile, contribute less than 10 percent.

As Table 8.3 shows, the huge preponderance of the movement in the real effective exchange rate is attributable to real shocks for the Japanese yen. Real shocks account for almost all of the movement in the real effective exchange rate at every horizon. Less than one percent of the variance is attributable to nominal shocks. The estimates imply that real shocks explain most of the variance in the real effective exchange rate.

According to forecast error variance decompositions for the nominal exchange rate, real shocks explain most of the movement here,

Table 8.2. Forecast Error Variance Decomposition with the Bivariate System: US Dollar.

Horizon (months)	Real shock (%)	Nominal shock (%)
(a) Real Effective Exchange Rate		
3	97.727	2.273
6	97.715	2.285
9	97.715	2.285
12	97.715	2.285
18	97.715	2.285
24	97.715	2.285
36	97.715	2.285
(b) Nominal Effective Exchange Rate		
3	90.417	9.583
6	90.408	9.592
9	90.408	9.592
12	90.408	9.592
18	90.408	9.592
24	90.408	9.592
36	90.408	9.592

as well. Real shocks explain more than 99 percent of the variance in the nominal effective exchange rate. Nominal shocks, meanwhile, contribute less than one percent.

To summarize, real shocks explain most of the forecast error variance of the movements in real and nominal exchange rates for the euro, US dollar, and Japanese yen. However, the influence of real shocks on the movements in real and nominal effective exchange rates may be somewhat stronger for the euro and Japanese yen than for the US dollar.

8.4. Trivariate System

8.4.1. *Empirical Techniques*

Next, we extend the bivariate model to a trivariate VAR model consisting of the first difference of output, real exchange rates, and

Table 8.3. Forecast Error Variance Decomposition with the Bivariate System: Japanese Yen.

Horizon (months)	Real shock (%)	Nominal shock (%)
(*a*) Real Effective Exchange Rate		
3	99.771	0.229
6	99.771	0.229
9	99.771	0.229
12	99.771	0.229
18	99.771	0.229
24	99.771	0.229
36	99.771	0.229
(*b*) Nominal Effective Exchange Rate		
3	99.482	0.518
6	99.482	0.518
9	99.482	0.518
12	99.482	0.518
18	99.482	0.518
24	99.482	0.518
36	99.482	0.518

nominal exchange rates. Consider the following infinite-order vector moving average (VMA) representation:

$$\Delta x_t = C(L)\varepsilon_t, \tag{8.6}$$

where L is a lag operator, Δ is a difference operator, $\Delta x_t = [\Delta y_t, \Delta r_t, \Delta e_t]'$ is a (3×1) vector of endogenous variables, and $\varepsilon_t = [\varepsilon_{s,t}, \varepsilon_{d,t}, \varepsilon_{n,t}]'$ is a (3×1) vector of structural shocks with covariance matrix Σ. The error term can be interpreted as supply shocks ($\varepsilon_{s,t}$), real demand shocks ($\varepsilon_{d,t}$), and nominal shocks ($\varepsilon_{n,t}$). The structural shocks are assumed to have no contemporaneous correlation or autocorrelation. This implies that Σ is a diagonal matrix.

To implement the econometric methodology, we need to estimate the following finite-order VAR model:

$$[I - \Phi(L)]\Delta x_t = u_t, \tag{8.7}$$

where $\Phi(L)$ is a finite-order matrix polynomial in the lag operator and u_t is a vector of disturbances. If the stationarity condition is satisfied, we can transfer equation (8.7) to the VMA representation:

$$\Delta x_t = A(L)u_t, \tag{8.8}$$

where $A(L)$ is a lag polynomial.

Equations (8.6) and (8.8) imply a linear relationship between ε_t and u_t:

$$u_t = C_0 \varepsilon_t. \tag{8.9}$$

C_0 in equation (8.9) is a 3×3 matrix defining a contemporaneous structural relationship to be identified for the vector of structural shocks ε_t in order to recover that vector from the estimated disturbance vector u_t. We need nine parameters to convert the residuals from the estimated VAR into the original shocks driving the behavior of the endogenous variables. Following Clarida and Gali (1994) and Hamori and Hamori (2008b), we impose three additional restrictions on the long-run multipliers while freely determining the short-run dynamics. These three restrictions are as follows:

(1) Nominal (monetary) shocks have no long-run impact on the levels of output;
(2) Nominal (monetary) shocks have no long-run impact on the real exchange rate;
(3) Real demand shocks have no long-run impact on the levels of output.

The long-run representation of equation (8.7) can be written as:

$$\begin{bmatrix} \Delta y_t \\ \Delta r_t \\ \Delta e_t \end{bmatrix} = \begin{bmatrix} C_{11}(1) & C_{12}(1) & C_{13}(1) \\ C_{21}(1) & C_{22}(1) & C_{23}(1) \\ C_{31}(1) & C_{32}(1) & C_{33}(1) \end{bmatrix} \begin{bmatrix} \varepsilon_{s,t} \\ \varepsilon_{d,t} \\ \varepsilon_{n,t} \end{bmatrix}, \tag{8.10}$$

where $C(1) = C_0 + C_1 + C_2 + \cdots$ are long-run multipliers of the structural VAR (long-run effect of ε_t on Δx_t). Based on the method of Clarida and Gali (1994), we stipulate that the long-run multipliers C_{12}, C_{13} and C_{23} are equal to zero, thus making the matrix $C(1)$ a lower triangular matrix.

The analysis in this chapter differs, in several respects, from the analyses from the existing papers such as Clarida and Gali (1994) and Hamori and Hamori (2008b). To begin with, this chapter uses the effective exchange rate, while Clarida and Gali (1994) and Hamori and Hamori (2008b) use bilateral exchange rates. Second, the system in this chapter consists of the output level, real effective exchange rate, and nominal effective exchange rate, while the system from Clarida and Gali (1994) and Hamori and Hamori (2008) consists of the relative output level, real bilateral exchange rate, and relative price level.

8.4.2. *Empirical Results*

When the SBIC is used to choose the optimal lag length of VAR in empirical analysis, the VAR(1) model turns out to be the most appropriate for all three countries. On this basis, we go on to calculate the forecast error variance decompositions.

Table 8.4 shows the fraction of the forecast error variance attributable to each shock at different horizons in the trivariate model for each variable for the euro area. Real supply shocks account for most of the forecast error variance of output throughout the estimation horizons. The rest of the variance is attributable to demand and nominal shocks. The estimates imply that real supply shocks explain most of the variance in output movements.

Forecast error variance decompositions for the movement in the real effective exchange rate suggest that real demand shocks explain most of the movement in the real exchange rate. Real demand shocks, the most important factors, account for more than 86 percent of the real exchange rate variance. Real supply shocks, meanwhile, account for about 12.9 percent of the forecast error variance. The nominal shocks of the real effective exchange rate explain less than one percent. To summarize, real demand shocks account for much of the forecast error variance of the movement in the real effective exchange rate.

Finally, forecast error variance decompositions for nominal effective exchange rates show that real demand shocks are responsible for about 88 percent of variation in the changes of nominal effective exchange rates. Real supply shocks and nominal shocks account for the rest of the variance.

Table 8.4. Forecast Error Variance Decomposition with the Trivariate System: Euro.

Horizon (months)	Real supply shock (%)	Real demand shock (%)	Nominal shock (%)
(*a*) *Output*			
3	91.868	6.878	1.253
6	91.399	7.175	1.427
9	91.398	7.175	1.427
12	91.398	7.175	1.427
18	91.398	7.175	1.427
24	91.398	7.175	1.427
36	91.398	7.175	1.427
(*b*) *Real Effective Exchange Rate*			
3	12.902	86.733	0.365
6	12.897	86.735	0.368
9	12.898	86.734	0.368
12	12.898	86.734	0.368
18	12.898	86.734	0.368
24	12.898	86.734	0.368
36	12.898	86.734	0.368
(*c*) *Nominal Effective Exchange Rate*			
3	11.148	88.140	0.712
6	11.139	88.149	0.712
9	11.139	88.149	0.712
12	11.139	88.149	0.712
18	11.139	88.149	0.712
24	11.139	88.149	0.712
36	11.139	88.149	0.712

Table 8.5 shows the fraction of the forecast error variance attributable to each shock at different horizons in the trivariate model for each variable for the United States. Real supply shocks explain most of the variance forecast error of output throughout the estimation horizons. Demand and nominal shocks account for the rest of the variance.

Forecast error variance decompositions for the variations in the real effective exchange rate suggest that real demand shocks explain most

Table 8.5. Forecast Error Variance Decomposition with the Trivariate System: US Dollar.

Horizon (months)	Real supply shock (%)	Real demand shock (%)	Nominal shock (%)
(a) Output			
3	99.522	0.369	0.109
6	99.521	0.370	0.109
9	99.521	0.370	0.109
12	99.521	0.370	0.109
18	99.521	0.370	0.109
24	99.521	0.370	0.109
36	99.521	0.370	0.109
(b) Real Effective Exchange Rate			
3	1.719	96.165	2.116
6	1.719	96.154	2.128
9	1.719	96.154	2.128
12	1.719	96.154	2.128
18	1.719	96.154	2.128
24	1.719	96.154	2.128
36	1.719	96.154	2.128
(c) Nominal Effective Exchange Rate			
3	1.350	89.474	9.175
6	1.350	89.466	9.184
9	1.350	89.466	9.184
12	1.350	89.466	9.184
18	1.350	89.466	9.184
24	1.350	89.466	9.184
36	1.350	89.466	9.184

of the movement in the real effective exchange rate. Real demand shocks, the most important factors, account for more than 96 percent of the real exchange rate variance. Real supply shocks, meanwhile, explain only about 1.7 percent of the forecast error variance. Nominal shocks account for about two percent of the real effective exchange rate variance. To summarize, real demand shocks account for much of the forecast error variance of the movement in the real effective exchange rate.

Forecast error variance decompositions for nominal effective exchange rates indicate that real demand shocks are responsible for about 90 percent of the variation in the changes of nominal effective exchange rates. Real supply shocks and nominal shocks account for about 10 percent of the variance.

Table 8.6 shows the fraction of the forecast error variance attributable to each shock at different horizons in the trivariate model for each variable for Japan. Real supply shocks account for most of the

Table 8.6. Forecast Error Variance Decomposition with the Trivariate System: Japanese Yen.

Horizon (months)	Real supply shock (%)	Real demand shock (%)	Nominal shock (%)
(*a*) *Output*			
3	95.084	1.594	3.323
6	95.049	1.597	3.354
9	95.049	1.597	3.354
12	95.049	1.597	3.354
18	95.049	1.597	3.354
24	95.049	1.597	3.354
36	95.049	1.597	3.354
(*b*) *Real Effective Exchange Rate*			
3	10.630	89.136	0.234
6	10.630	89.136	0.234
9	10.630	89.136	0.234
12	10.630	89.136	0.234
18	10.630	89.136	0.234
24	10.630	89.136	0.234
36	10.630	89.136	0.234
(*c*) *Nominal Effective Exchange Rate*			
3	11.048	88.458	0.494
6	11.049	88.457	0.494
9	11.049	88.457	0.494
12	11.049	88.457	0.494
18	11.049	88.457	0.494
24	11.049	88.457	0.494
36	11.049	88.457	0.494

variation in the forecast errors of output. Demand and nominal shocks account for rest of the variance. The estimates imply that real supply shocks explain most of the variance of output movements.

Forecast error variance decompositions for the variations in the real effective exchange rate suggest that real demand shocks explain most of the movement in the real exchange rate. Real demand shocks, the most important factors, account for more than 89 percent of the variance. Real supply shocks, meanwhile, account for about 10.6 percent of the forecast error variance in the real effective exchange rate. Nominal shocks account for less than one percent of the variance. To summarize, real demand shocks are responsible for much of the forecast error variance of the movement in the real effective exchange rate.

Forecast error variance decompositions for nominal effective exchange rates show that about 88 percent of variation in the changes of nominal effective exchange rates is explained by the real demand shocks. The rest of the variance is accounted for by real supply shocks and nominal shocks.

To summarize, real shocks (real supply and real demand shocks) explain most of the forecast error variance of the movements in the real and nominal exchange rates for the euro area, the United States, and Japan. However, the influence of real shocks on the movements in real and nominal effective exchange rates may be somewhat stronger in the euro area and Japan than in the United States. These results are consistent with the results obtained from the bivariate system (Tables 8.1, 8.2, and 8.3).[2]

8.5. Some Concluding Remarks

This chapter examines the sources of real and nominal effective exchange rate fluctuation of the euro, US dollar, and Japanese yen using a long-run structural VAR approach. After identifying two

---

[2]We carried out a similar analysis using the relative output (the difference between the output of each country and the output of advanced countries) instead of the output itself. Then we obtained similar results.

types of macroeconomic shocks (real and nominal), we uncover the sources driving the movements in real exchange rates. The evidence presented indicates that real shocks are the dominant explanatory factors behind the real and nominal effective exchange rate fluctuations of the euro, US dollar, and Japanese yen. Real disturbances account for more than 99 percent of the forecast error variance in the real and nominal effective exchange rates for the euro and Japanese yen. Real disturbances account for more than 97 percent of the forecast error variance in the real effective exchange rate and more than 90 percent of the nominal effective exchange rate for the US dollar. These results are consistent with those of Lastrapes (1992), Enders and Lee (1997), and Hamori and Hamori (2007). Our results also suggest that the influence of real shocks on the movements in real and nominal effective exchange rates is somewhat stronger in the euro area and Japan than in the United States.

Next, we extend the model to identify three types of macroeconomic shocks (real supply, real demand, and nominal) in order to reveal the sources driving the movements in real exchange rates. Once again, our empirical results indicate that real shocks (real demand and real supply) are the dominant explanatory factors behind the real and nominal effective exchange rate fluctuations. Real disturbances account for more than 98 percent and 99 percent of the forecast error variance in the real and nominal effective exchange rates respectively, in the euro area and Japan, and more than 97 percent and 90 percent of the forecast error variance in the real and nominal effective exchange rates respectively, in the United States. Again, the influence of real shocks on the movements in real and nominal effective exchange rates may be relatively more important in the euro area and Japan than in the United States. These results are consistent with the results obtained by the bivariate SVAR model.

Euro Area Enlargement

9.1. Introduction

The EU is currently witnessing an expansion trend. Ten countries, namely, Cyprus, the Czech Republic, Estonia, Hungary, Latvia, Lithuania, Malta, Poland, Slovakia, and Slovenia, were included in May 2004 followed by two more, namely, Bulgaria and Romania, in January 2007. The EU membership has increased to include 27 countries. Croatia — the former Yugoslav Republic of Macedonia — and Turkey are candidates for EU membership and negotiations toward this end have begun. In line with this trend, the Economic and Monetary Union (EMU) has also seen its ranks grow with the inclusion of Greece in January 2001, Slovenia in January 2007, Cyprus and Malta in January 2008, and Slovakia in January 2009. With the EMU having expanded to include 16 countries, from the original 11 in 1999, the euro area is gradually expanding.

Participation in the EMU implies adopting the euro as the participating country's sole currency and allowing the country's interest rates to be set by the European Central Bank (ECB) based on the overall economic condition of the euro area. In addition, EMU member states ought to abide by all the terms and conditions of the EU's Stability and Growth Pact.

As discussed in Chapter 1, participation in the EMU and adoption of the euro as the sole currency requires compliance with the following economic convergence criteria provided in Article 121.1 of the Maastricht Treaty, formally known as the Treaty on European Union (the Treaty).

(1) Price Stability: During the year preceding the evaluation, the average rate of increase in consumer prices must not exceed that

of the three EU member states with the lowest rates of inflation by more than 1.5 percent.[1]

(2) Long-term Interest Rate Stability: During the year preceding the evaluation, the average long-term government bond yield must not exceed that of the three EU member states with the lowest rates of inflation by more than two percent.

(3) Government Deficits: The annual government (central government, regional governments, and social security accounts) deficit must not exceed three percent of the nominal GDP or it must be continuously declining in real terms and must be close to the three percent criterion. Further, the annual government deficit in excess of three percent of the nominal GDP must be exceptional and temporary.

(4) Government Debt: The government debt must not be more than 60 percent of the nominal GDP or must be in the process of declining to the 60 percent level at a sufficient rate.

(5) Exchange Rate Stability: The country's currency must maintain the Exchange Rate Mechanism (ERM) exchange rate fluctuation margins over the most recent two years of European Monetary System (EMS) membership, without devaluations.

In addition to the above-mentioned criteria, countries must achieve legal convergence. In other words, as stipulated by Articles 108 and 109 of the Treaty and the Statute of the European System of Central Banks (ESCB), countries must revise their central bank laws and other related laws in order for them to be consistent with laws stipulated in the Maastricht Treaty and Statute of the ESCB.

The European Central Bank (ECB) and the European Commission prepare Convergence Reports biennially in accordance with Article 122.2 of the Maastricht Treaty in order to assess the status of economic convergence of the countries that have not adopted the euro. However, a country that has not adopted the euro can request for the assessment of its progress in achieving economic convergence — a condition

---

[1] The assessment period for the initial group of countries joining the EMU was the year ending on 31 December 1997. For countries joining afterward, assessment periods have been provided in Convergence Reports of the European Commission and the European Central Bank.

for participating in the final stage of the EMU. Subsequently, the assessment is carried out and Convergence Reports are prepared.

In this chapter, we review the background and current status of euro area enlargement and consider its future prospects. We analyze (1) the countries that were EU member states when the euro as a single currency was adopted in January 1999, but were not participants in the final stage of the EMU and (2) the countries that became EU members after adopting the euro. We refer to the former as the "existing EU member state group" and the latter as the "accession countries".

9.2. Existing EU Member State Group

9.2.1. *Greece*

Greece was included in the EU in 1981 and was keen to participate in the third and final stage of the EMU as part of the initial group; however, as of the end of 1997, it failed to meet the participation criteria. Consequently, it undertook various measures aimed at ensuring EMU participation as early as possible.

First, in order to meet the exchange rate criterion, it adopted the ERM in March 1998 and the ERM II when it was launched in January 1999. Greece also implemented a reduction in indirect taxes between October 1998 and December 1999, thus successfully lowering prices, containing wage increases, and restraining inflation expectations in the process. Further, beginning in August 1998, gentlemen's agreements signed between the government and commercial and industrial enterprises and service providers were effective in maintaining and stabilizing retail prices. These agreements covered one-tenth of the CPI basket in 1998 and one-third in 1999. Needless to say, monetary tightening and fiscal austerity policies were also implemented.

In March 2000, Greece requested the ECB and the European Commission to carry out the assessment of its compliance with the criteria for participating in the final stage of the EMU. The ECB and the European Commission carried out the assessment and reported their conclusions in the 2000 Convergence Report as described below. During the reference period of April 1999 to March 2000, Greece was found to be in compliance with price stability, long-term interest rate, exchange rate stability, and government deficit criteria. However, it was not found to be in compliance with the government debt criterion.

With respect to consumer price inflation (the 12-month Harmonised Index of Consumer Prices [HICP] average rate of inflation), Greece was found to have an inflation rate of two percent, as opposed to the reference value of 2.4 percent. The report attributed this result to the policies mentioned above and to the need to lower international oil prices.[2] However, because (1) the inflation rate exceeded the euro area's average rate of 1.4 percent and (2) the price-lowering impacts of domestic policies were considered to be temporary, the report also cited the importance of maintaining price stabilization policies.

Greece was found to have a long-term interest rate of 6.4 percent, as opposed to the reference value of 7.2 percent. Compared to the average long-term interest rate of the euro area in March 2000, the difference was approximately 0.8 percent.

With respect to exchange rate stability, the report found that Greece, which had adopted the ERM and ERM II over the previous two years, had maintained its currency — the drachma — within the exchange rate fluctuation margin established for that period and had not implemented any devaluations.

Greece was found to have a general government deficit to GDP ratio of 1.6 percent, as compared to the reference value of three percent in 1999 and 1.3 percent (projected) in 2000. However, the report found Greece to have a debt to GDP ratio of 104.4 percent in 1999 and 103.7 percent (projected) in 2000; although these results reflected steady improvement, the values were still high as compared to the reference value of 60 percent. The report stated that for Greece to rapidly approach the reference value, it would have to promote social security system reforms, privatization of government enterprises, and other structural reforms; maintain fiscal austerity policies; and eliminate government deficits or generate surpluses, while abiding by the provisions of the Stability and Growth Pact.

---

[2]See European Central Bank (2000).

With respect to legal convergence, Greece implemented revisions in the Statute of the Bank of Greece and other laws in 2000, thus achieving consistency with the Statute of the ESCB.

Based on the assessment findings, the European Commission recommended that Greece be allowed to participate in the final stage of the EMU. After consultation in the European Parliament, deliberation by the European Council, comprising EU heads of state, and finally, approval of more than 50 percent of the members of the Economic and Financial Affairs (ECOFIN) Council — the council meeting comprising finance ministers, Greece was made the twelfth participant in the final stage of the EMU in January 2001. The euro-drachma exchange rate was set at 1 euro = 340.750 drachmas.

9.2.2. *Denmark*

Denmark was included in the EU in 1973 together with the UK and Ireland. In May 1992, the Danish parliament approved the Maastricht Treaty by a vote of 125 to 25, and in accordance with the Danish constitution, the treaty was put to a vote of Danish citizens in June of the same year; however, it was rejected by 51 percent of the voters. After the rejection of the Danish referendum, the Edinburgh European Council, held in December 1992, took the unusual step of approving EMU opt-out clauses for Denmark and the UK with respect to the following aspects of Article 122: (1) common currency, (2) security and defense, (3) judicial and home affairs cooperation, and (4) EU citizenship. This was done to promote treaty implementation.[3] Both Denmark and the UK agreed to hold national referendums on all or some of the opt-outs at appropriate times in the future.

In May 1993, the Maastricht Treaty was again put to a national vote in Denmark, and this time, it was ratified by 57 percent of the voters.

Despite this, a September 2000 national referendum[4] resulted in voters rejecting Denmark's participation in the final stage of the EMU by a 53 percent majority, and leaving the issue concerning the

---

[3]When the Maastricht Treaty took effect, implementation under the same conditions by all EU member states became necessary.

[4]Voter turnout was 87 percent.

adoption of the euro unresolved. In the end, these elections raised concern over not only the economic advantages and disadvantages of adopting the euro single currency but also social problems such as the decline of the social welfare system and the possibility of an increase in immigration from Central and Eastern Europe, which voters feared would result from EU participation. It is also said that an emotional debate centered on the concern over the loss of Denmark's identity as an independent nation had undue influence on the outcome of the voting. Nevertheless, with conditions substantially different from those in the UK and Sweden (discussed below), it can be said that Denmark is the most eligible of the three countries for EMU participation.

We summarize the details of EMU opt-out clauses exercised by Denmark with respect to the common currency as follows:

(1) Denmark's participation in the final stage of the EMU will be premised on the results of a national referendum on the same. Consequently, even if Denmark meets the criteria for EMU participation, it will not be obligated to automatically adopt the euro and will participate in the final stage of the EMU only after a formal request submitted by its government.[5]

(2) Denmark will not be bound by the economic policy rules applicable to EMU participants. The monetary policies of Denmark's central bank — the Danmarks Nationalbank — will be implemented in accordance with the national laws and regulations and will not be bound by the Treaty or the Statute of the ESCB.

(3) Denmark will participate in the second stage of the EMU and maintain a fixed exchange rate system based on the ERM of the EMS.

(4) Denmark may pursue its own fiscal policies with regard to income distribution and social welfare. Similar to the countries that have adopted the euro, the Danish government supports fiscal discipline under the Stability and Growth Pact. However, even if Denmark develops a fiscal deficit that exceeds the reference value

---

[5]As in the case of Greece, EMU participation will be formally recognized after the completion of certain EU-level procedures.

of three percent of the nominal GDP, the disciplinary provisions of the Stability and Growth Pact will not be applicable to it.

In contrast to the UK and Sweden, Denmark was already in compliance with the participation criteria, including the requirement of two years of ERM adoption, by the time the first group of participants in the final stage of the EMU was determined. Furthermore, in compliance with the EMU opt-out clause mentioned above, Denmark adopted ERM II when it was launched to replace the ERM when the euro was introduced in 1999. The Danish central bank, therefore, had to maintain the exchange rates of Denmark's currency — the krone — within an exchange rate fluctuation margin of ±2.25 percent of the central rate versus the euro.[6] This implies that the Danish central bank has to maintain its own monetary policy in line with that of the ECB and has very little room for implementing discretionary monetary policy actions. Despite this, however, Denmark has no right to involve itself in the ECB's monetary policy setting process. Therefore, whenever the ECB has implemented interest rate hikes, Denmark's central bank has had to raise its interest rate in order to maintain an exchange rate in line with that of the ERM II. As a result, Denmark's inflation and interest rates have approximated those of euro area countries. Subsequently, Denmark, like the UK and Sweden, enjoys economic fundamentals (economic growth rate, unemployment rates, and inflation rate), which are basically strong, as compared to those of euro area countries (See Table 9.1), and this strength has, conversely, become one reason for it not participating in the EMU.

Although a certain number of administrative procedures are required at the EU level, in Denmark's case, euro adoption will be effectively determined once it is approved in a referendum. Therefore, the focus of attention is when and under what sort of conditions the next referendum will take place. When Prime Minister Rasmussen emerged victorious in Denmark's November 2007 general elections, he declared

---

[6]The currencies of ERM II participants are permitted to fluctuate at ±15 percent versus the central for the euro. However, because Denmark is regarded as having achieved a high degree of economic convergence, it and the ECB agreed to apply a narrower fluctuation margin of ±2.25 percent for the Danish currency in 1998.

Table 9.1.   Summary Statistics.

	Denmark	Sweden	UK	Euro Area
Economic Growth Rates				
1999	2.56	4.60	3.04	2.44
2000	3.53	4.40	3.80	3.98
2001	0.70	1.06	2.37	3.86
2002	0.47	2.41	2.05	0.90
2003	0.38	1.91	2.77	0.78
2004	2.30	4.13	3.26	1.84
2005	2.44	3.30	1.84	1.68
2006	3.34	4.09	2.84	2.87
2007	1.65	2.58	3.17	2.95
Unemployment Rates				
1999	5.70	5.58	4.16	9.36
2000	5.40	4.68	3.60	8.37
2001	4.78	3.98	3.20	8.02
2002	4.88	3.98	3.09	8.29
2003	5.67	4.85	3.02	8.84
2004	5.85	5.52	2.76	8.89
2005	5.60	7.12	2.73	8.50
2006	3.81	7.04	2.97	7.83
2007	3.30	6.12	2.70	7.12
Inflation Rates				
1999	2.06	0.55	1.35	1.12
2000	2.71	1.29	0.80	2.17
2001	2.30	2.67	1.22	2.37
2002	2.38	1.93	1.27	2.29
2003	1.98	2.34	1.36	2.07
2004	0.90	1.02	1.34	2.15
2005	1.70	0.82	2.05	2.19
2006	1.85	1.50	2.33	2.18
2007	1.67	1.68	2.32	2.14

Source: International Financial Statistics (International Monetary Fund).

that he would subject participation in the final stage of the EMU to a referendum within four years. Amid the global economic downturn resulting from the global financial instability which began in 2007 with the sub-prime loan problem in the US and which has been worsening since the fall of 2008, the economic condition of Denmark has also worsened. If they become noticeably worse than the conditions in euro area countries, there is a strong possibility that a national referendum or other concrete steps toward euro adoption will be taken. As discussed above, there is basically no opposition to euro adoption within the Danish government or the central bank or other policy authorities, which are already effectively conducting fiscal and monetary policies in a manner that is consistent with the policy actions of euro area countries. On the contrary, great expectations are attached to EMU participation and the consequent gaining of rights to contribute to policy setting of the euro area. However, to the extent that Denmark could be considered to already be included in the euro area, Danish citizens may have greater-than-expected feelings of opposition toward abandoning their country's currency which is considered as a symbol of Denmark's national identity. In this sense, there still exist significant uncertainties regarding the possible results of a referendum.

9.2.3. *The UK*

The UK, which became a member of the EU in 1973, has always drawn a clear line between itself and continental countries — chiefly France and Germany — that have promoted EU integration in not only economic areas such as tariffs, trade, capital, and labor but also areas like currency, taxation, politics, and defense which are directly related to national identity. In 1992, the UK, together with Denmark, was given access to EMU opt-out clauses as a condition of their ratifying the Maastricht Treaty. In the case of the UK, specifics relating to one of those clauses — those concerning the common currency — are summarized as follows:

(1) Even if the UK satisfies the EMU participation criteria, it is not obligated to automatically adopt the euro and will participate in the final stage of the EMU only if its government submits a request for the same.[7]

---

[7]EMU participation will be formally approved once certain EU-level procedures are completed.

(2) The UK will pursue monetary policies in accordance with its own laws. Consequently, it will not be bound by the Treaty or the Statute of the ESCB. The UK's central bank — the Bank of England — will implement its monetary and exchange rate policies with the goal of stabilizing prices under a floating rate system. The Bank of England will implement inflation targeting with a goal of maintaining inflation at two percent.

(3) The UK will not be not subject to the fiscal deficit provisions of the Maastricht Treaty.

The British government, while acknowledging that the success of a single currency in the single European market will lead to trade, cost transparency, and currency stability benefits for both Europe and the UK, formally declared in October 1997 that it will not participate in the final stage of the EMU. At the same time, it announced its policy concerning the EMU. The UK premised its participation in the final stage of the EMU on: (1) decisions by the British government and parliament to pursue that route and approval in a national referendum,[8] (2) complete compliance with the EMU participation criteria, and (3) passing of five economic tests established by the UK treasury. The purpose of the five economic tests was to objectively and unambiguously determine whether economic conditions would permit the UK to enjoy the benefits of EMU participation. These five tests concerned the following:

(1) Convergence: The establishment of an environment in which the UK could accept the interest rates applicable to the euro area without suffering disadvantages requires substantial progress in the convergence of business cycles and economic structures with the euro area in the long term. The degree of progress in convergence will be measured using economic indicators like inflation rates, interest rates, economic growth rates, and effective exchange rates.

(2) Flexibility: In order for the British economy to absorb asymmetric shocks that may arise as a result of EMU participation, it is

---

[8] The holding of national referendums shall be performed in accordance with the UK's laws.

necessary, in particular, for there to be sufficiently high flexibility and mobility in labor markets and for appropriate fiscal policies to be implemented.

(3) Investment: As a result of EMU participation, long-term expansions in domestic and outward investment must take place.

(4) Financial Services: As a result of EMU participation, the international competitiveness of the UK's financial services industry and the City wholesale market, in particular, must increase and must be profitable.

(5) Growth, Stability, and Employment: As a result of EMU participation, the UK's economic growth and stability and employment must be advanced.

In a 1997 assessment by the UK treasury, it was judged that none of the five economic tests had been successfully completed. In other words, it was determined that convergence had not been achieved between the UK and the euro area to take shape in 1999 and that flexibility was insufficient, resulting in inadequate sustainable and durable convergence. As such, it was concluded that even if the UK was to participate in the EMU, it would risk not being able to enjoy investment, growth, employment promotion, and other such benefits.

In June 2003, the UK treasury performed another assessment. This time, it was found that although the UK's economy had been progressing significantly with respect to completing the five economic tests since 1997, all the tests had not been completed. For three tests, namely, investment; financial services; and growth, stability, and employment, it was determined that the conditions sufficient for obtaining substantial benefits from EMU participation had been achieved. However, for the remaining two tests, namely, convergence and flexibility, the assessment found the conditions to be inadequate. In other words, the assessment indicated that the UK still lacked economic convergence and flexibility required for successfully addressing and absorbing unforeseen difficulties or shocks in the wake of its adoption of the euro.

Since the 2003 assessment results of each of the five economic tests are useful in understanding the British government's stance on the

EMU, we provide their simple summaries. Beginning with investment, it was considered that if the EMU were managed well and the UK was participating under appropriate conditions, the foreign direct investment would expand in the long term. Delays in participating in the EMU, therefore, would lead to the risk of forgoing the benefits to be obtained from expanded investment in the UK. EMU participation was also considered to be highly likely to result in lower long-term interest rates and lower procurement costs for companies. Further, if sustainable and durable convergence could be achieved, investment would improve in terms of both quantity and quality, and the criterion would be met. With regard to financial services, wholesale financial service firms entered the UK in droves after the EMU was launched and maintained a high level of competitiveness for its wholesale financial service industry. EMU participation, therefore, would most certainly allow the industry to enjoy additional profits and further solidify its position. Alternatively, extended delays in participating in the EMU would work to forego these benefits. In sum, the financial services criterion was met. With respect to growth, stability, and employment, it was expected that EMU participation would permit the UK to enjoy expanded euro area trade and lower prices as well as significant increase in production and personal income. Moreover, achieving sustainable and durable convergence would result in the meeting of this criterion. With regard to convergence, the UK was found to have met the Treaty's convergence criteria — a condition for EMU participation — in terms of its inflation rate, long-term interest rates, government deficit, and government debt. However, significant structural gaps with the euro area countries still existed in areas like the housing market. Further, it was unclear whether or not the economic cycle convergence was sufficient for permitting the UK to smoothly manage its economy under euro area interest rates. Consequently, although the degree of convergence was considered to have clearly risen, it was not considered sufficient to meet the convergence criterion. Finally, with regard to flexibility, the UK's labor market had made significant improvement in terms of flexibility, resulting in a considerably lower rate of unemployment and substantial employment expansion. Indeed, the UK had the lowest unemployment rate in the EU. Nevertheless, for the British economy to be able to absorb risks and asymmetric shocks resulting from EMU participation and to hold production and employment instability to a minimum, additional efforts to boost flexibility and resilience are required. Sufficient flexibility would also be necessary for facilitating the achievement of sustainable and durable convergence. In general, the results indicated that the UK economy had yet to reach a stage at which it could be considered prepared in terms of flexibility.

The sustainable and durable convergence between the UK and the euro area was one criterion for determining that the UK economy had passed three of the five economic tests. In other words, sustainable and durable convergence was a key condition that had to be met before the UK could enjoy the potential benefits of EMU participation. In order to determine whether this key condition had been met, it was sufficient to simply ascertain whether the convergence test, which was one of the five economic tests, had been passed. In other words, if the UK economy did not meet the convergence criterion, it would be impossible for it to pass all the five economic tests. To realize sustainable and durable convergence, the British government asserted that it would implement the following four policies: (1) Have the Bank of England adopt inflation targets based on HICP being used by the euro area; (2) Undertake housing market functional improvements aimed at stabilizing housing demand and supply and reforming the long-term home loan market; (3) Pursue fiscal stability through the establishment of a fiscal base for implementing discretionary fiscal policies; and (4) Embark on market reforms aimed at increasing flexibility in labor, capital, and product markets.

To participate in the EMU, the UK must adopt the ERM II, and it has not changed its negative stance on this requirement for fear of suffering a significant loss in its fiscal policy independence. The UK had adopted the ERM II's predecessor, the ERM. Before the UK adopted the ERM, it had been suffering from inflation which it had tried to address by implementing a high interest rate policy. However, the efforts proved to be futile, and its economy sank into recession. To help control its inflation, the UK won the right to implement fixed exchange rates that would cause the pound trade at higher-than-market rates as a condition for its adopting the ERM in October 1990. This policy worked to control inflation as planned. However, the Deutsche Bundesbank — the central bank of Germany — which was a key-currency country, had been pursuing a tight-money policy to prevent inflation related to the unification of East and West Germany. Thus, it was difficult for the UK to implement significant interest rate cuts to maintain the ERM fixed exchange rate, and as a result, its economy sank into recession. In the summer of 1992, a currency crisis, referred to as the sterling crisis, emerged and hedge funds seized on it as an opportunity to massively reduce the pound. To maintain the ERM fixed exchange rate, the Bank of England desperately intervened to support the pound; however, in the end, it was left with no choice but to quit the ERM. When this happened in September 1992, the pound crashed. This bitter experience is considered to be one reason behind the UK's negative stance on adopting the ERM II. Even if the UK formally decides to adopt the ERM II in the future, it will not be possible for it to meet the EMU participation criteria unless it can maintain the pound within the exchange rate fluctuation margin versus the euro for at least two years.

Since the euro was introduced in 1999, the UK's economic performance has been significantly better than that of the euro area (see Table 9.1). As such, it has not been easy to gain public support for adopting the euro, and no time limit has been set for government and parliamentary decisions or a national referendum. Having said that, global financial anxieties, which took a turn for the worse in the fall of 2008, have had a major impact on the UK — the center of global financial services. It appears that the UK's economy shrank by 0.7 percent in 2008 and that the economic conditions are rapidly worsening. The British government ratified the EU's Reform Treaty (also known as the Treaty of Lisbon) in both the upper and lower houses of parliament without resorting to a national referendum in a clear indication of its support for further EU enlargement and integration and of its stance that under the right economic conditions, euro adoption would have significant benefits for the UK. It is believed, therefore, that if the UK treasury, in its next assessment of progress in meeting the five economic tests, determines that the UK's economy has met the criteria for all five, including convergence, the UK will adopt the euro. Although it is unclear when this might happen, judging from the fact that the previous assessment in 2003 was conducted six years after the one prior to that in 1997, the next assessment could take place within a few years, if steady progress has been made on the reforms that the government had called for in 2003. If the UK's economy is found to have passed all five economic tests in the next assessment, there is a high possibility that concrete moves toward government and parliamentary approval and a national referendum on participating in the final stage of the EMU will be observed.

9.2.4. *Sweden*

Of the existing EU member state group, Sweden was the last to be included in the EU, having done so in 1995 after the Maastricht Treaty had taken effect. Therefore, unlike Denmark and the UK, Sweden cannot make use of the treaty's EMU opt-out clauses. This implies that it must automatically adopt the euro once it meets the participation criteria for the final stage of the EMU.

As of the end of 1997, Sweden had met the EMU participation criteria except for the requirement to make its currency — the krona — part of the ERM. It also had yet to revise its central bank laws and implement other necessary legal measures. Owing to this, Sweden's participation as an initial member of the EMU was not recognized. This outcome was the result of Sweden's own decisions as described below and differed fundamentally from the case of Greece which desperately wanted to participate in the EMU but could not meet the participation criteria. Unable to gain the support of the Swedish people at that time, the Swedish government and parliament judged that it was too early to adopt the euro and postponed ERM adoption. The Swedish central bank — the Sveriges Riksbank — pursued monetary and exchange rate policies in accordance with Sweden's central bank laws, maintaining its independence in both the policy areas. In 1995, it also adopted an inflation target of a 2 percent ± 1 percent annual increase in the CPI for achieving the policy purpose of maintaining stable prices under a floating exchange rate system.

In November 2002, the government announced that a national referendum[9] on EMU participation would be held in September of the following year, and undertook a major PR campaign to obtain approval. Involved in this campaign were the ruling Social Democratic Party and three other political parties, namely, the Moderate, Liberal, and Christian Democratic parties, along with the Confederation of Swedish Enterprise, the main trade unions, and the majority of Sweden's media. Opinions, however, differed between and within political parties and three opposition parties with seats in parliament — the Left, Centre, and Green parties — opposed euro adoption. Furthermore, within the ruling Social Democratic government, while the Prime Minister actively supported EMU participation, five cabinet members publicly opposed it. Owing to the divided opinions on EMU participation, voters rejected it by a majority of 56 percent in the September 2003 national referendum. This result, similar to that of the Danish referendum, was more a reflection of concern about the loss of national identity and other political factors than simply about economic issues.

According to the ECB's Convergence Report,[10] Sweden, barring its lack of adoption of the ERM II launched in 1999, and adoption of floating exchange rates, met the criteria for participating in the final stage of the EMU during the period of 2006–2008. To adopt the euro, Sweden must gain parliamentary and voter approval, and meet the criteria for participating in the EMU. This implies that it must adopt the ERM II for at least two years, maintain its currency — the krona — within the exchange rate fluctuation margin versus the euro, and undertake the required revisions of its central bank and other laws. Considering that the krona-euro exchange rate fluctuation range was -1.6 percent–$+0.3$ percent over the past three years, within the exchange rate fluctuation margin stipulated for ERM II participants, it is anticipated that if Sweden approves of the ERM II participation, it will face no

---

[9]Sweden has no constitutional provisions requiring a national referendum as a condition for EMU participation. All of its political parties, however, have pledged to abide by the results of national referendum when deciding whether to support EMU participation.

[10]See European Central Bank (2006b) and European Central Bank (2008a).

procedural hurdles for euro adoption at the EU level. Be that as it may, however, Sweden's economic performance since the euro came into being has been better than that of euro area countries (see Table 9.1), and the difficulty of obtaining voter support for euro adoption under such economic circumstances, together with the impact of Sweden's previous experience with a national referendum on EMU participation discussed above, makes it difficult to expect Sweden to move forward with either government approval or a national referendum.

Nevertheless, there are some indications of change in Sweden's stance of distancing itself from the EMU. To begin with, the September 2006 general elections ended the 12-year rule of the left-wing Social Democratic Party in favor of a right-wing coalition government led by the Moderate Party, and was said to basically favor euro adoption. Additionally, amid a global financial crisis and recession that worsened in 2008, the krona, which is subject to floating exchange rates, experienced a greater loss of value than the euro. Sweden's economy is suffering in other ways as well, and if it appears to become significantly weaker than the euro area economies, it is possible that the country will take concrete steps toward joining the final stage of the EMU.

9.3.   Accession Countries

Countries that joined the EU after the euro came into being are referred to as the "accession countries." These countries are not permitted to adopt the euro immediately and must meet the applicable Maastricht Treaty (the Treaty on European Union; the Treaty) requirements after attaining EU membership. Other stipulations include participation in the ERM II for at least two years and the maintenance of an exchange rate fluctuation margin versus the euro. The Treaty, therefore, requires that countries achieve a high degree of sustainable, long-term economic convergence before they can advance from stage one, i.e., EU membership, to stage two, i.e., participation in the final stage of the EMU and euro adoption.

The 12 accession countries include Bulgaria, Cyprus, the Czech Republic, Estonia, Hungary, Latvia, Lithuania, Malta, Poland, Romania, Slovakia, and Slovenia. These countries can be divided into two groups: (1) those that have already achieved EMU participation — Slovenia, Cyprus, Malta, and Slovakia — and (2) those that have not.

The latter[11] are not participating in the EMU because they have not fulfilled all the participation requirements set forth in Article 121.1 of the Maastricht Treaty and are referred to as "member states with derogations". The rights and responsibilities related to euro adoption — certain Maastricht treaty provisions and certain ECB system rights and responsibilities — are not applicable to these countries. These member states with derogations are transitioning from socialist to capitalist economies, are in the process of liberalizing prices and introducing the private ownership of property, and are characterized by economic growth rates that are relatively high compared to those of the existing EU member state group. Additionally, while they are not EMU participants, some (Estonia, Latvia, and Lithuania) are ERM II participants and others (Bulgaria, the Czech Republic, Hungary, Poland, and Romania) are neither EMU participants nor ERM II participants.

Below, we describe certain conditions pertaining to three groups of accession countries — those that are EMU participants, those that are ERM II participants, and those who are not ERM II participants.

9.4. EMU Participants

Of the countries included in the EU in 2004 or later, Slovenia, Cyprus, Malta, and Slovakia have obtained EMU participation. All four of these countries were included in the EU on 1 January 2004. Each is briefly addressed below in the order in which they were included in the EMU.

9.4.1. *Slovenia*

Slovenia requested the ECB and European Commission to assess its compliance with participation criteria for the final stage of the EMU

---

[11] Sweden is included among the member states with derogations and is covered in Convergence Report assessments together with the accession countries that are member states with derogations.

in March 2006. Both the organizations documented their assessments of Slovenia's compliance with the Treaty's provisions with regard to inflation, fiscal condition, exchange rates, long-term interest rates, and legal convergence in their Convergence Reports.[12]

During the April 2005 to March 2006 reference period, Slovenia was found to have an average inflation rate of 2.3 percent, a figure lower than the reference value of 2.6 percent. It was considered to not only have stable prices supported by a sound economic foundation but also to require continued efforts to maintain low inflationary conditions and competitive advantage through the use of tools like cautious fiscal policies and appropriate wage increases.

With respect to Slovenia's fiscal condition, its 2005 fiscal deficit was only 1.8 percent of its GDP which was well below the reference value of three percent. This outcome resulted from a combination of improving economic conditions and cautious fiscal policies. Slovenia also had a 2005 government debt-to-GDP ratio of less than 30 percent which was significantly below the reference value of 60 percent. Under its convergence plan, Slovenia is aiming to reduce its government deficit to one percent of the GDP in 2008, and it was pointed out that it will have to announce various concrete belt-tightening policies in order to achieve this.

With respect to exchange rates, Slovenia has been an ERM II participant since June 2004. Its ERM II participation, therefore, began before the start of the required two-year period, and it had maintained its currency — the tolar — within the exchange rate fluctuation margin versus the euro.

Slovenia's average long-term interest rate during the reference period was 3.8 percent, less than the reference value of 5.9 percent. That Slovenia had maintained its long-term interest rate within 0.1 percent–0.7 percent of the long-term interest rate of the euro area (long-term government bond yield), since it joined the ERM II in June 2004, signified the steady progress it had made in its convergence process.

With respect to legal convergence, Slovenia's laws were found to be consistent with the Treaty and the Statute of the ESCB. In other words,

---

[12]See European Central Bank (2006b).

the inconsistencies mentioned in the 2004 Convergence Reports[13] were found to have been taken care of through legal revisions.

As summarized above, Slovenia was determined to meet the convergence criteria. Further, since both the ECB and the European Commission drew similar assessment conclusions, the latter recommended that Slovenia be permitted to adopt the euro. Following approval by the European Parliament, deliberation by EU heads at the European Council, and approval by a majority of the ECOFIN Council, Slovenia became the 13th country to be included in the final stage of the EMU on 1 January 2007, and the tolar-euro exchange rate was set at 1 euro = 239.640 tolars.

9.4.2. *Cyprus*

In February 2007, the governments of Cyprus and Malta requested for the assessment of their compliance with the participation criteria for the final stage of the EMU, and, similar to the case of Slovenia, the ECB and the European Commission documented their assessment results in separate Convergence Reports which are discussed below.[14]

To begin with, Cyprus was determined to have an average inflation rate of two percent during the April 2006–March 2007 reference period, a figure lower than the reference value of three percent. The realization of stable prices in Cyprus had been supported by wage discipline and the promotion of competition in some product markets and by the effects of EU-participation-induced integration with the single market and globalization. The report stated that Cyprus will have to be wary of potentially strengthening inflationary pressures arising from further convergence and lowering of interest rates following euro adoption. Furthermore, it was recommended that its government should maintain cautious fiscal policies to keep excessive demand at bay and bring about wage hikes that are consistent with productivity increases.

---

[13] See European Central Bank (2004).
[14] See European Central Bank (2007).

With regard to its fiscal condition, Cyprus was determined to have a 2006 fiscal deficit of only 1.5 percent of the GDP, which was significantly below the reference value of three percent, and was expected to lower it even further in 2007 and later. Its government debt, on the other hand, began falling as a percentage of GDP in 2005, but was still at 65.3 percent, which was higher than the reference value of 60 percent, in 2006. However, the expectation that this figure would decline to 61.5 percent in 2007 supported the judgment that steady declines in the reference values were being achieved. It was pointed out that for Cyprus to achieve its convergence plan, it would be important for it to achieve even greater fiscal soundness by restraining the outlays for public pensions through the implementation of measures like pension reforms.

With regard to exchange rates, Cyprus had been an ERM II participant since May 2005 and was a member for the required two years at the time of the adoption of the Convergence Reports in May 2007. Over this period, the Cypriot pound traded at rates slightly high against the euro central rate, but was kept within the exchange rate fluctuation margin.

During the reference period, the average long-term interest rate in Cyprus was 4.2 percent which was less than the reference value of 6.4 percent. In addition, in the previous two to three years, the gap between the reference value and the long-term interest rate of the euro area had narrowed, which indicated gradual convergence progress by Cyprus and a declining country risk.

With respect to legal convergence, it was noted that revisions of the Central Bank of Cyprus Law and other laws deemed necessary in the prior Convergence Reports[15] had been made. As a result, Cypriot laws were determined to be consistent with the Maastricht Treaty and the Statute of the ESCB.

Given the above, Cyprus was determined to be in compliance with the convergence criteria and after the implementation of procedures similar to those applied to Slovenia, Cyprus was officially approved for euro adoption beginning on 1 January 2008. The final Cypriot

---

[15]See European Central Bank (2004, 2006b).

pound-euro exchange rate was set at 1 euro = 0.585274 Cypriot pounds.

9.4.3. *Malta*

Assessment results for Malta are described below.[16]

Malta's average inflation rate for the April 2006–March 2007 reference period was found to be 2.2 percent which was below the reference value of three percent. The country's achievement of stable prices, as in the case of Cyprus, was supported by wage discipline and the promotion of competition in some product markets, with help from the effects of EU-participation-induced integration with the single market and globalization. It was pointed out that Malta could not afford to let its guard down against a growing risk of inflation as its economy recovered. It was also judged that Malta should maintain its cautious fiscal policy stance to avoid excessive demand and wage increases, and move forward with structural reforms to improve market functions.

With respect to its fiscal condition, Malta's 2006 fiscal deficit was found to be 2.6 percent of the GDP and less than the reference value of three percent. However, its government debt to GDP ratio, despite having declined since 2004, was still at 66.5 percent which was above the reference value of 60 percent in 2006. However, Malta had been gradually reducing its fiscal deficit since it was included in the EU in 2004, and was judged to also be steadily reducing its government debt toward the reference value. The assessment results also mentioned that the Maltese government must without doubt move forward with health insurance and other reforms and continue its efforts to achieve long-term, sustainable improvements in its fiscal condition.

Further, with respect to exchange rates, Malta had been an ERM II participant since May 2005 and was a participant for the required two years when the Convergence Reports were adopted in May 2007. Over this period, its currency — the lira — remained extremely stable, trading near the euro central rate.

---

[16]See European Central Bank (2007).

Malta's average long-term interest rate during the reference period came in below the 6.4 percent reference value at 4.3 percent. The country's success in bringing its long-term interest rate closer to that of the euro area since 2005 was considered as an indication of its steady progress in convergence and a declining country risk.

As for legal convergence, the implementation of the revised Central Bank of Malta Act in February 2007 resulted in consistency between Malta's laws and the Treaty and the Statute of the ESCB.

Based on the results described above, Malta, too, was concluded to have met the convergence criteria. Following the implementation of procedures similar to those applied to Slovenia, Malta, like Cyprus, was formally approved to adopt the euro on 1 January 2008. The lira-euro exchange rate was finally set at 1 euro = 0.429300 lira. The inclusion of Cyprus and Malta brought the total number of EMU member states up to 15.

9.4.4. *Slovakia*

The Slovakian government requested an assessment of its compliance with the participation criteria for the final stage of the EMU in April 2008. As in the cases of the three countries covered above, the ECB and European Commission prepared separate Convergence Reports[17] describing their assessment findings. The results are discussed below.

During the April 2007–March 2008 reference period, Slovakia had an average inflation rate of 2.2 percent, which was lower than the reference value of 3.2 percent. The assessments concluded that Slovakia must continue to remain vigilant against inflation, promote wage setting in accordance with productivity increases, and move ahead with structural reforms for improving product market functions.

With respect to its fiscal condition, Slovakia had a 2007 fiscal deficit to GDP ratio of 2.2 percent, a figure below the reference value of three percent and was expected to fall even lower in 2008. In addition, its 2007 government debt to GDP ratio at 29.4 percent

---

[17]See European Central Bank (2008a).

was significantly better than the reference value of 60 percent. Given the expectation that Slovakia would see increased tax revenues due to economic growth, the assessment results cited the importance of actively strengthening the country's fiscal base. Specifically, the assessment results indicated that Slovakia should progress to achieve the medium-term objective of lowering the fiscal deficit-to-GDP ratio below one percent by 2010. The European Commission recommended to the Council of the European Union that the excessive deficit procedure, or EDP, initiated for Slovakia be discontinued, and this move was formally approved in June. Thus, Slovakia could meet the EMU participation criteria concerning fiscal conditions.

With respect to exchange rates, Slovakia had been an ERM II participant since November 2005 which sums up to more than the required two years. However, while its currency — the koruna — had remained within the exchange rate fluctuation margin, it experienced a strong appreciation of eight to nine percent in terms of the euro central rate between July 2006 and March 2007, causing the ERM II koruna-euro central rate to be raised by 8.5 percent on 19 March 2007. Subsequently, until January 2008, the koruna traded at 3 percent–7.3 percent above the new central parity. During the two-year reference period, the koruna was traded at an average of 5.4 percent above the euro central rate, but within the exchange rate fluctuation margin, supporting the judgment that this was a healthy development reflecting Slovakia's positive economic conditions.

Slovakia's average long-term interest rate of 4.5 percent during the reference period was lower than the reference value of 6.5 percent. Slovakia had been rapidly reducing the gap between its long-term government bond yield, a representative long-term interest rate and that of the euro area since 2002, before it was included in the EU. Its success in doing so was considered as an indication of its gradual convergence progress and a declining country risk.

With regard to legal convergence, Slovakia's laws were determined to be consistent with both the Treaty and the Statute of the ESCB.

Given the above results, Slovakia was concluded to have met the convergence criteria. After the completion of procedures like those performed for the three countries discussed above, Slovakia was formally approved to become the sixteenth EMU member state on 1 January 2009. The koruna-euro exchange rate was finally set at 1 euro = 30.1260 koruna (SKK).

9.5. ERM II Participants

The countries that are not yet participating in the EMU but are participating in the ERM II include Estonia, Latvia, and Lithuania which share national borders with one another. Together, they are referred to as the three Baltic States and are considered as promising candidates for the next round of euro adoption.

The three Baltic States easily meet the EMU participation criteria for long-term interest rates, fiscal condition, and exchange rates (see Table 9.2). They have also made steady progress on legal convergence and revising central bank and other laws, and Estonia and Lithuania have already completed this process.

The only EMU participation criterion that the three Baltic States are struggling with is the one concerning price stability (see Table 9.2). According to the Convergence Reports produced by the ECB and European Commission for 2008,[18] Estonia's HICP inflation rate for the April 2007–March 2008 reference period was 8.3 percent, Latvia's was 12.3 percent, and Lithuania's was 7.4 percent. All of them significantly exceeded the reference value of 3.2 percent. The factors giving rise to these exceptionally high inflation rates were common to all three Baltic States. Examples include rising wage costs and increasing domestic demand, both driven by economic growth, hikes in managed prices and excise taxes in connection with liberalization, and sudden rise in global prices of oil, other energy, and food. The three countries were expected to experience even higher inflation by the end of 2008, with some relief beginning perhaps as early as 2009, as a result of economies cooling amid the global recession. The relatively low price level in these three Baltic States (about 60 percent of the EU average in 2006), however, introduces the possibility of price level convergence in the long run.

---

[18]See European Central Bank (2008a) and European Commission (2008).

Table 9.2.   Overview Table Economic Indicators of Convergence.

| | | Price stability | Government budgetary position | | | Exchange rate | | Long-term interest rate |
		HICP inflation[1]	Country in excessive deficit	General government surplus(+) or deficit(−)[2]	General government gross deficit[2]	Currency participating in ERM II	Exchange rate vis-à-vis euro[3,4]	Long-term interest rate[1]
Bulgaria	2006	7.4		3.0	22.7	No	0.0	4.2
	2007	7.9	No	3.6	18.2	No	0.0	4.5
	2008	9.2	No	3.2	14.1	No	0.0[3]	4.7[1]
Czech Republic	2006	2.1	Yes	−2.7	29.4	No	4.8	3.8
	2007	3.0	Yes	−1.6	28.7	No	2.0	4.3
	2008	4.4	No	−1.4	28.1	No	8.4[3]	4.5[1]
Estonia	2006	4.4	No	3.4	4.2	Yes	0.0	—(6)
	2007	6.7	No	2.8	3.4	Yes	0.0	—(6)
	2008	8.3[1]	No	0.4	3.4	Yes	0.0[3]	—(6)
Latvia	2006	6.6	No	−0.2	10.7	Yes	0.0	4.1
	2007	10.1	No	0.0	9.7	Yes	−0.5	5.3
	2008	12.3[1]	No	−1.1	10.0	Yes	0.4[3]	5.4[1]

(Continued)

Table 9.2. (*Continued*)

		Price Stability	Government budgetary position			Exchange rate		Long-term interest rate
		HICP inflation[1]	Country in excessive deficit	General government surplus(+) or deficit(−)[2]	General government gross deficit[2]	Currency participating in ERM II	Exchange rate *vis-à-vis* euro[3,4]	Long-term interest rate[1]
Lithuania	2006	3.8	No	−0.5	18.2	Yes	0.0	4.1
	2007	5.8	No	−1.2	17.3	Yes	0.0	4.5
	2008	7.4[1]	No	−1.7	17.0	Yes	0.0[3]	4.6[1]
Hungary	2006	4.0	Yes	−9.2	65.6	No	−6.5	7.1
	2007	7.9	Yes	−5.5	66.0	No	4.9	6.7
	2008	7.5[1]	Yes	−4.0	66.5	No	−2.7[3]	6.9[1]
Poland	2006	1.3	Yes	−3.8	47.6	No	3.2	5.2
	2007	2.6	Yes	−2.0	45.2	No	2.9	5.5
	2008	3.2[1]	No	−2.5	44.5	No	6.3[3]	5.7[1]
Romania	2006	6.6	—	−2.2	12.4	No	2.6	7.2
	2007	4.9	No	−2.5	13.0	No	5.4	7.1
	2008	5.9[1]	No	−2.9	13.6	No	−10.3[3]	7.1[1]

(*Continued*)

170 Introduction of the Euro and the Monetary Policy of the ECB

Table 9.2. (*Continued*)

	Price Stability	Government budgetary position			Exchange rate		Long-term interest rate
	HICP inflation[1]	Country in excessive deficit	General government surplus(+) or deficit(−)[2]	General government gross deficit[2]	Currency participating in ERM II	Exchange rate vis-à-vis euro[3,4]	Long-term interest rate[1]
Slovakia 2006	4.3	Yes	−3.6	30.4	Yes	3.5	4.4
2007	1.9	Yes	−2.2	29.4	Yes	9.3[5]	4.5
2008	2.2[1]	No	−2.0	29.2	Yes	2.5[3]	4.5[1]
Reference value[7]	3.2%	No	−3.0%	60%	Yes	±15%	6.5%

Sources: European Commission (Eurostat) and ECB.

(1) Average annual percentage change. 2008 data refers to the period April 2007 to March 2008.
(2) As a percentage of GDP. European Commission spring 2008 forecast for 2008.
(3) Average annual percentage change. Data for 2008 are calculated as a percentage change of the average over the period 1 January 2008 to 18 April 2008 compared with the average of 2007.
(4) A positive number denotes an appreciation *vis-à-vis* the euro and a negative number a depreciation *vis-à-vis* the euro.
(5) With effect from 19 March 2007 the central rate of the Slovak koruna in ERM II was revalued by 8.5 percent.
(6) For Estonia no long-term interest rate is available.
(7) The reference value refers to the period April 2007 to March 2008 for HICP inflation and for long-term interest rates, and to the year 2007 for general government balance and general government debt.

Economic conditions in each of the three Baltic States are briefly discussed below.

Estonia: After joining the ERM II in June 2004, Estonia adopted its own currency board arrangement and strictly maintained the value of its currency — the kroon — in terms of the euro central rate. A currency board arrangement is the strictest type of fixed exchange rate system. In its currency board arrangement, Estonia has hard pegged the kroon against the euro central rate,[19] has limited the amount of kroons in circulation, basically to the level of its foreign currency reserves, and has guaranteed the exchangeability of kroons and euros. The Estonian Central Bank — the Easti Pank — has abandoned its own discretionary monetary policies and instead follows those of the ECB. Estonia's long-term government bond yield cannot be determined because the country has issued almost no long-term government bonds. Estonia is extremely sound fiscally, having recorded fiscal surpluses before it joined the EU, and its ratio of government debt to GDP remained extremely low, in single digits (3.4–5.3 percent), over the period 2002–2008. Using bank loan interest rates as a substitute for long-term interest rates, the ECB and European Commission have determined that Estonia is within the reference value criterion for long-term interest rates.[20] Estonia would like to become an EMU participant as early as possible and originally planned to achieve this objective in 2008. However, given an inflation rate far above the reference value, it postponed its application and is now expected to achieve the EMU participation in 2011.

Latvia: Latvia joined the ERM II in May 2005 and has adopted its own exchange rate peg to the euro in which it has maintained its currency — the lats — in a highly narrow exchange rate fluctuation margin of ±1 percent versus the euro central rate. An exchange rate peg is an ordinary fixed exchange rate, and in Latvia's case, its central bank — the Bank of Latvia — intervenes to maintain parity in the value of the lats

---

[19]Estonia began using a currency board as early as 1992 when it pegged the kroon against the Deutsche mark and then the euro.

[20]See European Central Bank (2008a) and European Commission (2008).

versus the euro. Latvia has employed a Special Drawing Rights (SDR) basket before it joined the ERM II and implemented its exchange rate peg versus the euro in January 2005. The country, however, has often entered into lats transactions at rates exceeding the central rate but within its own narrow central rate ±1 percent exchange rate fluctuation margin. Latvia, which maintains that it would like to join the EMU as early as possible, originally planned to do so in 2008, but postponed its application because of an inflation rate that significantly exceeded the reference value. At present, it is said that it is aiming to achieve EMU participation in 2012.

Lithuania: Lithuania became an ERM II participant in June 2004 and adopted a currency board arrangement under which it zealously maintained the value of its currency — the litas — against the euro central rate. Beginning in April 1994, it used the US dollar for this arrangement and later, in February 2002, switched to the euro. Aiming to be included in the EMU in January 2007, Lithuania requested the ECB and European Commission to assess its compliance with euro adoption criteria in March 2006. During the April 2005–March 2006 reference period, however, the country had an average inflation rate that exceeded the reference value, although only by 0.1 percent, and was expected to witness higher inflation by the end of 2006. As a result, it was judged to have not met the price stability criterion and was not approved for euro adoption.[21] At present, it is said that Lithuania is aiming to achieve EMU participation in 2010 or as soon thereafter as possible.

As described above, among the three Baltic States, Estonia and Lithuania are a step ahead of Latvia which is slightly lagging in terms of legal preparation and progress toward market integration with the EU. For all three countries, it appears that the ability to control inflation rates and hold them below the reference value for EMU participation will be largely determined by changes in exchange rate management direction, in other words, by determining whether the three Baltic States can effectively abandon the extremely strict fixed

---

[21] See European Central Bank (2006a).

exchange rate systems (currency boards and exchange rate pegs) that they have embraced for many years, and accept their currencies rising by as much as 10 percent against the euro central rate under the exchange rate fluctuation margins recognized under the ERM II. Slovakia is an example of a country that was able to absorb the Balassa–Samuelson effect[22] and limit inflation through the appreciation of its currency. The Balassa–Samuelson effect is a phenomenon in which international competition causes wage increases in the high-productivity traded goods sectors of a low-income country and those increases themselves bring about wage increases in low-productivity non-traded goods sectors resulting in across-the-board price increases. In other words, this is a situation in which rising productivity and economic growth in a low-income country in the midst of an economic catch-up result in rising inflation. The impact of the Balassa–Samuelson effect on inflation when Lithuania's euro adoption was rejected became a topic of debate.

9.6. Countries that are not ERM II Participants

Bulgaria, the Czech Republic, Hungary, Poland, and Romania are not ERM II participants. The common characteristic of these five countries is that, among the accession countries, their economies are relatively large. In addition, because they are not ERM II participants, they will each require at least two years, in principle, to fulfill the participation criteria for the final stage of the EMU. We summarize the conditions and problems in each of these countries, based on assessments in the 2008 Convergence Reports prepared by the ECB and European Commission (see Table 9.2).

Bulgaria: Bulgaria became an EU member in January 2007. Its first ECB and European Commission assessments were reported in the 2008 Convergence Reports issued by those institutions. The assessments found that for the April 2007–March 2008 reference period, Bulgaria's HICP average inflation rate was 9.4 percent, significantly exceeding the reference value of 3.2 percent and preventing the

---

[22]See Chapter 6 in Mulhearn and Vane (2008).

country from meeting this EMU participation criterion. The reasons behind Bulgaria's high inflation rate were found to be the same as those behind the high inflation rate of the three Baltic States, and it was expected that Bulgaria would enter a period of declining inflation in 2009. Bulgaria's fiscal condition was judged to be extremely strong and in compliance with the EMU participation criteria. The country was not specified as an EDP target. In 2007, Bulgaria had a fiscal surplus equal to 3.4 percent of the GDP, and it was expected to maintain surpluses for 2008 and later. Additionally, in 2007, Bulgaria's government debt came to only 18 percent of the GDP, significantly below the reference value of 60 percent. With regard to exchange rates, Bulgaria adopted a currency board arrangement in July 1997. In doing so, it began to strictly manage its currency — the lev — against the Deutsche mark, and when Germany gave up the Deutsche mark in favor of the euro, it maintained strict management practices against the euro central rate as it does even now. Bulgaria adopted this currency board arrangement to stabilize its macro economy and has achieved some measure of success in doing so. Moving on, Bulgaria was found to have an average long-term interest rate of 4.7 percent which, being below the reference value of 6.5 percent, met the long-term interest criterion. Finally, with respect to legal convergence, Bulgaria, despite having implemented revisions to the Law on the Bulgarian National Bank and other laws in 2007, was determined to be in legal conflict with Articles 108 and 109 of the Treaty and with the Statute of the ESCB. Desiring to achieve formal participation in the ERM II as quickly as possible, Bulgaria is said to be aiming for euro adoption in 2011, and inflation is likely to be the key hurdle in doing so. With respect to the ERM II minimum participation period, it is possible that the country's use of a currency board arrangement for managing the lev against the euro will be considered in some form.

The Czech Republic: The assessment results for the Czech Republic are described below. During the April 2007–March 2008 reference period, the Czech Republic was found to have an HICP average inflation rate of 4.4 percent which exceeded the reference value of 3.2 percent and prevented it from fulfilling this EMU criterion. After joining the EU in 2004, the Czech Republic enjoyed relatively stable prices and an inflation rate below the reference value. Beginning in the latter half of 2007, however, global energy and food prices began to rise sharply and, together with consumption tax and managed price hikes, resulted in upward inflation pressure that, it is believed, could not be fully absorbed by increases in the value of the Czech Republic's currency, the koruna. The country's inflation rate is expected to fall below three percent in 2009, and the Czech Republic's central bank — the Czech National Bank — is working to implement an inflation targeting policy that would seek to keep inflation at 3 percent ± 1 percent.[23] With regard to its fiscal condition, the Czech Republic was specified as an EDP target in 2004, but has since seen its fiscal deficits steadily decline to 1.6 percent of the GDP in 2007, well below the three percent reference value. The country's 2007 government debt to GDP ratio came to 28.7 percent, a level significantly lower than the reference value of 60 percent and was expected to decline even further in 2008. As such, the European Commission, in May 2008, recommended to the Council of the European Union that the EDP for the Czech Republic be discontinued, and this step was formally taken in June. Thus, the Czech Republic has met the EMU participation criteria regarding fiscal conditions. Turning to exchange rates, the Czech Republic employs a floating exchange rate regime in which the Czech National Bank intervenes to prevent large fluctuations in the koruna-euro exchange rate. To that extent, therefore, the Czech Republic should be considered to be using a managed float system. The koruna-euro rate has remained within the ERM II's central rate ±15 percent exchange rate fluctuation margin, with the koruna increasing by almost 13 percent against the euro during the two-year reference period (19 April 2006–18 April 2008). During the assessment reference period, the Czech Republic was found to have an average long-term interest rate of 4.5 percent which was below the reference value of 6.5 percent and which allowed the country to meet the long-term interest criterion. In the area of legal convergence, the Czech Republic revised its Act on the Czech National Bank, Act on the Financial Arbitrator, and other laws in 2007 but is still considered to have legal conflicts with Articles

---

[23] Between 2010 and euro adoption, an inflation rate of two percent is being targeted.

108 and 109 of the Treaty and with the Statute of the ESCB. Under a 2006 plan, the Czech Republic was targeting EMU participation to begin in January 2010 but it has since withdrawn that plan and has yet to set a new target.

Hungary: Hungary's assessment results are described below. For the April 2007–March 2008 reference period, Hungary was found to have not met the inflation criterion due to its HICP average inflation rate of 7.5 percent which exceeded the reference value of 3.2 percent. Hungary has experienced wide variations in its inflation rate which, at times, has never fallen below the reference value. The reasons for this are believed to have been similar to those impacting the three Baltic States, except that in Hungary's case, the effects of oil and food price fluctuations have been particularly significant. Fluctuations in the exchange rate for its currency — the forint — have also affected Hungary's inflation rate. Lower food and energy prices forecast for 2009 are expected to bring the inflation rate down to below four percent. Furthermore, since 2001, the Hungarian central bank — the Magyar Nemzeti Bank — has been pursuing an inflation targeting policy aimed at achieving an inflation rate of three percent over the medium term. With respect to its fiscal condition, the designation as an EDP target in 2004 spurred Hungary to embark on a fiscal consolidation program that began in the middle of 2006 and succeeded in increasing government revenues through enhanced tax collection and in lowering government expenditures. As a result, the country's fiscal deficit to GDP ratio declined from 9.2 percent in 2006 to 5.5 percent in 2007. This downward trend was predicted to continue, falling to 3.6 percent, a level approaching the reference value of three percent, in 2009. In contrast, Hungary's 2007 government debt was found to be 66 percent of its GDP, higher than the reference value of 60 percent and was expected to remain at that level for 2008 and 2009. The country, therefore, was found to not have fulfilled the fiscal condition criteria. With respect to exchange rates, Hungary adopted a euro peg in 2001 and maintained the forint within the exchange rate fluctuation margin of ±15 percent relative to the euro central rate. In February 2008, Hungary moved to a free-floating exchange rate. Over the two-year reference period (19 April 2006–18 April 2008), the forint-euro exchange rate fluctuation margin was −6.6 percent–+7.7 percent, and the forint marked an overall increase of approximately 4.5 percent against the euro. Hungary failed to meet the long-term interest rate criterion with an average long-term interest rate during the reference period of 6.9 percent versus the reference value of 6.5 percent. In fact, Hungary's long-term interest rate has been above the reference value since it became an EU member in 2004, and the gap with long-term government bond yields of the euro area has been widening, indicating that progress has not been made on convergence and that country risk is not declining. In the area of legal convergence, Hungary's central bank law — the Act on the Magyar Nemzeti Bank (MNB) — was revised in 2007. Despite that, however, legal inconsistencies remained between this law, the Statutes of the MNB, the Hungarian Constitution, and Hungary's Credit Institution Act, on the one hand, and Articles 108 and 109 of the Treaty and the Statute of the ESCB, on the other. As described above, Hungary was found to not have met certain EMU participation criteria, and no target date for euro adoption has been set. Compared to other member states with derogations, Hungary urgently needs decisive action with regard to administrative and economic reforms. It is anticipated that Hungary's move to a free-floating exchange rate will produce exchange rate variations that serve to absorb inflation pressures to some degree. It is believed that if Hungary can succeed in controlling its inflation, it can consider meeting the other participation criteria.

Poland: The assessment results for Poland are discussed below. During the April 2007–March 2008 reference period, Poland had an HICP average inflation rate of 3.2 percent, equaling the reference value. However, because of factors similar to those affecting the three Baltic States and other member states with derogations, Poland's inflation rate began to rise sharply in the second half of 2007, with an anticipated peak at 4.3 percent for 2008 before a projected decline to 3.4 percent in 2009. Amid expectations that its annual inflation rate would soon exceed the reference value, Poland was found to not have met the inflation rate criterion. The country's central bank — the National

Bank of Poland — has adopted an inflation targeting policy and is aiming to maintain inflation at 2.5 ± 1 percent. With respect to its fiscal condition, Poland was designated an EDP target in 2004, after which its fiscal deficit steadily decreased to two percent of the GDP in 2007, a level within the three percent reference value. Poland's government debt to GDP ratio, which came to 45.2 percent in 2007, easily beating the reference value of 60 percent, was expected to continue to decrease in 2008. At the request of the European Commission and the Council, Poland submitted a new convergence plan, including a medium-term fiscal reduction plan, in March 2008. Based on the assessment results for this plan and the fiscal deficit and government debt results mentioned above, it is possible that the European Commission will recommend to the Council the discontinuation of the EDP for Poland.[24] At present, however, the country has yet to fulfill the fiscal condition criteria. In the area of exchange rates, Poland has adopted a floating exchange rate regime. Over the two-year reference period (19 April 2006–18 April 2008), the exchange rate for Poland's currency — the zloty — fluctuated over a range of −4.8 percent–+13 percent against the euro, and marked an overall appreciation of nearly 13 percent. Poland's average long-term interest rate over the reference period came to 5.7 percent, staying under the reference value of 6.5 percent and allowing the country to meet the long-term interest rate criterion. On the matter of legal convergence, inconsistencies remained with Articles 108 and 109 of the Treaty and the Statue of the ESCB, despite the 2007 revision of Poland's Act on the National Bank of Poland. A target date for Poland's joining the EMU has yet to be set.

Romania: Romania became an EU member in January 2007 and underwent its first assessment by the ECB and European Commission for the Convergence Reports issued for 2008. For the April 2007–March 2008 reference period, Romania's HICP average inflation rate of 5.9 percent exceeded the reference value of 3.2 percent, preventing Romania from meeting this criterion. Though Romania's average inflation rate displayed a steep decline from approximately 15 percent

---

[24]The Council closed the EDP for Poland in July 2008.

in 2004 to 4.9 percent in 2007, this improvement was supported by the appreciation of Romania's currency — the leu — from 2004. Beginning in the latter half of 2007, drought-related crop failures and global market movements resulting in rapid agricultural commodity price increases and factors similar to those impacting the three Baltic States and other member states with derogations set inflation on an upward trend that was expected to continue till the end of 2008. Romania's central bank — the National Bank of Romania — has adopted an inflation targeting policy in which it aims to keep inflation in the range of ±1 percent around a disinflationary path. With respect to its fiscal condition, Romania is not the subject of an EDP. Its fiscal deficit for 2007 was determined to be 2.7 percent of the GDP and below the reference value of three percent. Nevertheless, with both revenues and expenditures trending upward over the past several years, the deficit to GDP ratio was expected to increase to 2.9 percent in 2008 and 3.7 percent in 2009. The government debt to GDP ratio, at 13 percent, was way below the reference value of 60 percent. This figure, too, however, was expected to gradually rise in 2008 and 2009. However, from an overall perspective, Romania was considered to have met the fiscal condition criteria. Moving on, Romania employs a floating exchange rate and, over the two-year reference period (19 April 2006–18 April 2008), the leu fluctuated over a range of −9.6 percent–+10.8 percent against the euro, appreciating by about 10 percent in the beginning of 2007, before depreciating about 15 percent. The causes for these wide swings in the exchange rate were determined to be a massive financial market confusion that emerged in the summer of 2007 and the following global recession. After joining the EU, Romania's long-term interest rate has remained above the reference value. During the reference period, it had an average long-term rate of 7.1 percent, versus the reference value of 6.5 percent. It did not, therefore, meet the long-term interest rate criterion. After Romania joined the EU, its long-term government bond yield narrowed the gap with the average for the euro area for a time, before beginning to widen in the second half of 2007 due to the impact of global financial instability. With respect to legal convergence, inconsistencies still existed in Articles 108 and 109 of the Treaty and the Statue of the ESCB, despite the 2004 implementation of a revised Romanian central bank law, the Law on the Statute of the BNR. Romania is now working to achieve euro adoption in 2014.

9.7. Outlook for the Future

Denmark, the UK, and Sweden, all of which were EU members prior to the introduction of the euro, can, either legally or in effect, determine when, if ever, they will adopt the euro, and all of them have thus far taken the stance that they will not. It is believed that Denmark will be the first of the three to do so, and that could happen within a few years. No estimations have been made on the adoption timing for the UK or Sweden.

As for the Central and Eastern European member states with derogations, all would like to achieve euro adoption as quickly as possible but none of them has met the EMU participation criteria. The most difficult of these to clear is the criterion concerning inflation. Within the EU accession countries involved in the processes of economic catch-up, the Balassa–Samuelson effect is considered to lead to a rise in the inflation rates. Indeed, the average economic growth rate in the 10 EU accession countries[25] over the period of 1999–2006 exceeded that of the 15 existing EU member states by four to five percent, and inflation in the accession countries over the years 1998–2006 was approximately two percent higher than that of the existing member states.[26] The calculations by De Grauwe and Schnabl (2005) indicate that the Balassa–Samuelson effect may be increasing inflation in the EU accession countries by one to three percentage points per year. The European Commission and ECB are aware of this and estimate that the Balassa–Samuelson effect accounts for an additional zero to two percentage points of inflation in the accession countries. An additional problem caused by the Balassa–Samuelson effect is that it interferes with the natural synergistic relationship between inflation control and exchange rate stability. In other words, countries in which the impact of the Balassa–Samuelson effect is

---

[25] Excluding Bulgaria and Romania, which joined the EU in 2007.
[26] According to Eurostat.

significant face extreme difficulties in both controlling inflation and stabilizing exchange rates, and must choose between the two. Among the Central and Eastern European member states with derogations, the Czech Republic, Hungary (except for its use of a euro peg from 2001 to February 2008), Poland, and Romania have made controlling inflation their highest priority, while Estonia, Latvia, Lithuania, and Bulgaria have chosen to stabilize exchange rates.

One stance in this debate advocates changing the manner in which the EMU participation inflation reference value is calculated and relaxing the criteria for participation in the single currency, so that the inflation impact of the Balassa–Samuelson effect on member states with derogations can be accounted for.[27] The gist of this position is that the admission of 12 new countries to the EU has resulted in an enlarged EU with economic conditions that have been changed or transformed relative to the time when the euro was first introduced and that the adjustment of the EU participation criteria to take into account the impact of the Balassa–Samuelson effect on accession countries should be flexibly considered. Both of the proposed changes below would respect the ECB principle of equal treatment:

(1) Calculate the inflation reference value not as the average for all EU member states, but as the average for the three states that have the lowest HICP average inflation rate among the states that have adopted the euro +1.5 percent.

(2) Calculate the inflation reference value based on the ECB inflation target. One of the ECB's policy objectives is to maintain an HICP inflation rate below but close to two percent. Allowing for a margin of +1.5 percent, the maximum reference value could be set at 3.4 percent (policy objective inflation rate of 1.9 percent + 1.5 percent).

Both these approaches would have resulted in a 2006 inflation reference value in excess of three percent and permitted Lithuania to meet the inflation criterion.

---

[27]For example, see Mulhearn and Vane (2008, Chapter 6) and Kennen and Meade (2003).

In response to views like this, the ECB and European Commission have taken the stance that there will be no changes in the EMU participation criteria to account for the Balassa–Samuelson effect.[28] Indeed, the Balassa–Samuelson effect is only one of the primary causes of inflation in the Central and Eastern European member states with derogations. These countries, therefore, rather than vainly focusing only on the Balassa–Samuelson effect, should basically work to control inflation at a pace appropriate for their own particular economic conditions. Given their current states of economic development, these countries should see euro adoption not as a near-term goal, but as a medium-to-long term goal and strive to achieve real convergence.

Considering the question of what should the Central and Eastern European member states with derogations do to realize euro adoption, we would like to make the following two recommendations.

The first is that the member states with derogations study the experiences of countries that have already achieved EMU participation and apply what they learn in their own policy management. For the member states with derogations, there should be much to be gained in this sense.

(1) Slovenia, Cyprus, and Malta: A common characteristic of all the three accession countries that achieved EMU participation is that their per capita incomes are close to the EU average. These countries, in other words, have succeeded to a relatively high degree in their economic catch-ups, and the impacts of the Balassa–Samuelson effect have been relatively small. Over the period of 1997–2008, Cyprus had an average per capita GDP equal to about 90 percent of the EU average, Malta's was about 80 percent, and Slovenia's was about 60 percent. In comparison, the average per capita GDP in the other accession countries came to about 55 percent of the EU average. Although Slovenia's per capita GDP was not particularly high compared to that of other accession countries over the subject time period, it grew at a faster rate after the country joined the EU in 2004. This indicates that one factor

---

[28]See European Central Bank (2008a) and Noyer (2001).

in achieving EMU participation is maintaining economic growth over a certain period and reaching a certain level of success with regard to economic catch-up.

(2) Slovakia: Slovakia's per capita income was not as high as that of the three countries discussed above, and was closer to that of the member states with derogations. The impact of the Balassa–Samuelson effect, therefore, should have been greater than what was experienced by the three countries above, but Slovakia succeeded in controlling inflation and cleared the reference value. This success is largely attributed to Slovakia's effective use of the exchange rate fluctuation margin of ±15 percent permitted under the ERM II. In other words, the country, by allowing its currency to trade at, or appreciate to, rates above the central rate but within the exchange rate fluctuation margin, was able to control rising prices for imported goods and relieve inflationary pressures brought about by the Balassa–Samuelson effect and other factors. It should be noted that the ECB and the European Commission approved an increase in the average value of Slovakia's currency against the euro in 2007. This shows that countries affected by the Balassa–Samuelson effect can themselves realize EMU participation by accepting a certain degree of exchange rate variation and focusing on controlling inflation. This can also be seen among the Central and Eastern European member states with derogations, where Poland, the Czech Republic, and other countries that have adopted inflation targets have achieved relatively stable prices and are close to clearing the inflation reference value.

(3) Greece, Spain, and Portugal: Within the EU, Greece, Spain, and Portugal had once found themselves in a position similar to that of the Central and Eastern European member states with derogations. However, they successfully met the criteria for participating in the final stage of the EMU and realized euro adoption by overcoming inflation causes other than the Balassa–Samuelson effect. In their cases, implementing balanced monetary and fiscal policy mixes and restraining effective wage increases were particularly effective in controlling inflation. These policies also proved effective in bringing about gradual catch-ups in real

incomes and progress in nominal convergence. The experiences of these countries, therefore, demonstrate the importance of sustained efforts to overcome inflation causes other than the Balassa–Samuelson effect for realizing EMU participation.

The second recommendation is that member states with derogations do what is necessary to achieve solid, sustainable economic convergence, in order to fully enjoy the merits of euro adoption. Specifically, these states must: (1) reform product, labor, and financial markets; (2) implement administrative reforms in areas like pensions and health insurance; (3) strengthen fiscal foundations; (4) enhance international competitiveness; and (5) work to improve long-term growth potential, employment, and productivity.

Finally, we would like to present our choice for the Central and Eastern European member states with derogations that are closest to achieving euro adoption. We believe the first closest group would include Estonia, Lithuania, and Latvia, all of which are already ERM II participants, and Bulgaria which has adopted a currency board. The second group would include the Czech Republic and Poland, both of which enjoy relatively stable prices.

If emphasis is to be placed on the stability of the euro's currency value and securing confidence in the euro, rapid euro area enlargement pursued to the extent of loosening euro adoption criteria is not an option. At the same time, intentionally closing the door to accession countries that are keen to adopt the euro would certainly not be beneficial for the EU. To date, the ECB and European Commission have employed extremely flexible interpretations regarding government debt as an aspect of fiscal condition when carrying out the assessments of countries wishing to adopt the euro, and have been flexible in approving ERM II exchange rate changes in terms of the euro central rate, given a legitimate economic reason. This stance should be maintained in the future. Countries that wish to adopt the euro, rather than rushing to do so, should steadily advance wide-ranging structural reforms addressing areas like labor and product markets, pensions and health insurance so that they can adopt the euro from a solid, sustainable position.

Panel FMOLS and Panel DOLS

Following Pedroni (2001), we briefly summarize the panel fully modified ordinary least squares (Panel FMOLS) method and panel dynamic ordinary least squares (Panel DOLS) method.

Consider the following co-integrating system for a panel:

$$y_{it} = \alpha_i + \beta_i x_{it} + u_{it} \quad i = 1, 2, \ldots, n : t = 1, 2, \ldots, T \quad \text{(A.1)}$$

$$x_{it} = x_{it-1} + v_{it}, \quad i = 1, 2, \ldots, n : t = 1, 2, \ldots, T \quad \text{(A.2)}$$

where $\varepsilon_{it} = (u_{it}, v_{it})$ is a stationary vector with long-run covariance matrix $\Omega_t = \lim_{T \to \infty} E[T^{-1}(\sum_{t=1}^{T} \varepsilon_{it})(\sum_{t=1}^{T} \varepsilon'_{it})]$. The long-run covariance can be estimated using HAC estimators. This covariance matrix can also be decomposed as $\Omega_t = \Omega_t^0 + \Gamma_t + \Gamma'_t$, where Ω_t^0 is the contemporaneous covariance and Γ_t is a weighted sum of autocovariances.

The between-dimension panel FMOLS estimator for the coefficient of β is given by

$$\hat{\beta}^{FM} = \frac{1}{N} \sum_{i=1}^{N} \left(\sum_{t=1}^{T} (x_{it} - \bar{x}_i)^2 \right)^{-1} \left(\sum_{t=1}^{T} (x_{it} - \bar{x}_i) y_{it}^* - T \hat{\tau}_i \right)$$

$$\text{(A.3)}$$

where

$$y_{it}^* = (y_{it} - \bar{y}_i) - \frac{\hat{\Omega}_{21i}}{\hat{\Omega}_{22i}} \Delta x_{it} \quad \text{(A.4)}$$

$$\hat{\tau}_i = \hat{\Gamma}_{21i} + \hat{\Omega}_{21i}^0 - \frac{\hat{\Omega}_{21i}}{\hat{\Omega}_{22i}} (\hat{\Gamma}_{22i} + \hat{\Omega}_{22i}^0) \quad \text{(A.5)}$$

We see that the panel FMOLS estimator given by (A.3) can be written as follows:

$$\hat{\beta}^{FM} = \frac{1}{N} \sum_{i=1}^{N} \hat{\beta}_i^{FM} \tag{A.6}$$

where $\hat{\beta}_i^{FM}$ is the FMOLS estimator for each member of the panel. Covariance and Γ_t is a weighted sum of autocovariances.

For the panel DOLS estimation, we need to augment the co-integrating regression (A.1) as follows:

$$y_{it} = \alpha_i + \beta_i x_{it} + \sum_{j=-K}^{K} \gamma_{ij} \Delta x_{it-j} + v_{it} \tag{A.7}$$

where v_{it} is the stationary error term. Then, the between-dimension panel DOLS estimator for the coefficient of β is given by

$$\hat{\beta}^{DOLS} = \frac{1}{N} \left[\frac{1}{N} \sum_{i=1}^{N} \left(\sum_{t=1}^{T} z_{it} z_{it}' \right)^{-1} \left(\sum_{t=1}^{T} z_{it} y_{it}^* \right) \right] \tag{A.8}$$

where $z_{it} = (x_{it} - \bar{x}_i, \Delta x_{it-K}, \dots, \Delta x_{it+K})$ is the $2(K+1) \times 1$ vector of regressors, and $y_{it}^* = y_{it} - \bar{y}_i$.

We see that the panel DOLS estimator given by (A.8) can be written as follows:

$$\hat{\beta}^{DOLS} = \frac{1}{N} \sum_{i=1}^{N} \hat{\beta}_i^D \tag{A.9}$$

where $\hat{\beta}_i^D$ is the conventional DOLS estimator, applied to the i-th member of the panel.

Bibliography

Ahmed, S. and Rogers, J. (1995). Government budget deficits and trade deficits: Are present value constraints satisfied in long-run data? *Journal of Monetary Economics*, 36, 351–374.

Artis, M. and Bayoumi, T.A. (1989). Saving, investment, financial integration and the balance of payments. IMF Working Paper.

Bekaert, G. and Hodrick, R. (2001). Expectations hypotheses tests. *Journal of Finance*, 56, 1357–1394.

Ball, L. (1999). Effective rules for monetary policy. *International Finance*, 2, 63–83.

Baltagi, B.H. (2005). *Econometric Analysis of Panel Data*, 3rd Ed. Chichester: John Wiley & Sons.

Bayoumi, T. and Eichengreen, B. (1992). Shocking aspects of European Monetary Unification. National Bureau of Economic Research Working Paper No. 3949.

Bayoumi, T.A. and Rose, A.K. (1993). Domestic saving and international capital flows. *European Economic Review*, 37, 1197–1202.

Bernanke, B. and Mihov, I. (1997). What does the Bundesbank target? *European Economic Review*, 41, 1025–1053.

Bhar, R. and Hamori, S. (2007). Analysing yield spread and output dynamics in an endogenous Markov switching regression framework. *Asia-Pacific Financial Markets*, 14, 141–156.

Blanchard, O. and Quah, D. (1989). The dynamic effects of aggregate demand and supply disturbances. *American Economic Review*, 79, 655–673.

Choi, I. (2001). Unit root tests for panel data. *Journal of International Money and Finance*, 20, 249–272.

Choi, S. and Wohar, M.E. (1991). New evidence concerning the expectations theory for the short-end of the maturity spectrum: 1910–1978. *Journal of Financial Research*, 14, 83–92.

Chowdhury, I.S. (2004). Sources of exchange rate fluctuations: Empirical evidence from six emerging market countries. *Applied Financial Economics*, 14, 697–705.

Clarida, R. and Gali, J. (1994). Sources of real exchange rate fluctuations: How important are nominal shocks? National Bureau of Economic Research Working Paper No. 4658.

Clarida, R., Gertler, M. and Galí, J. (1998). Monetary policy rules in practice: Some international evidence. *European Economic Review*, 42, 1033–1067.

Clarida, R., Gertler, M. and Galí, J. (2000). Monetary policy rules and macroeconomic stability: Theory and some evidence. *Quarterly Journal of Economics*, 115, 147–180.

Coenen, G. and Vega, J.L. (2001). The demand for M3 in the euro area. *Journal of Applied Econometrics*, 16, 727–748.

Coiteux, M. and Olivier, S. (2000). The saving retention coefficient in the long run and in the short run: Evidence from panel data. *Journal of International Money and Finance*, 19, 535–548.

Committee for the Study of Economic and Monetary Union (1989). Report on economic and monetary union in the European Community: Delors Report, Luxembourg: Official Publications of the European Communities (http://www.ena.lu/).

De Grauwe, P. and Schnabl, G. (2005). Nominal versus real convergence: EMU entry scenarios for the new member states. *Kyklos*, 58, 537–555.

Dekle, R. (1996). Saving-investment associations and capital mobility on the evidence from Japanese regional data. *Journal of International Economics*, 41, 53–72.

Deutsche Bundesbank (2005). The changes to the Stability and Growth Pact. *Monthly Report*, April, 15–21.

Dibooglu, S. and Kutan, A. (2001). Sources of real exchange rate fluctuations in transition economies: The case of Poland and Hungry. *Journal of Comparative Economics*, 29, 257–275.

Dickey, D.A. and Fuller, W.A. (1979). Distribution of the estimators for autoregressive time series with a unit root. *Journal of the American Statistical Association*, 74, 427–431.

Dornbusch, R. (1976). Expectations and exchange rate dynamics. *Journal of Political Economy*, 84, 1161–1176.

Enders, W. and Lee, B.S. (1997). Accounting for real and nominal exchange rate movements in the post-Bretton Woods period. *Journal of International Money and Finance*, 16, 233–254.

Estrella, A. and Hardouvelis, G.A. (1991). The term structure as a predictor of real economic activity. *Journal of Finance*, 46, 555–576.

Estrella, A. and Mishkin, F.S. (1997). The predictive power of the term structure of interest rates in Europe and the United States: Implications for the European Central Bank. *European Economic Review*, 41, 1375–1401.

European Central Bank (1998). *The Single Monetary Policy in Stage Three: General Documentation on ESCB Monetary Policy Instruments and Procedures.* Frankfurt am Main, Germany: European Central Bank.

European Central Bank (2000). *Convergence Report 2000.* Frankfurt am Main, Germany: European Central Bank.

European Central Bank (2002). *Convergence Report 2002.* Frankfurt am Main, Germany: European Central Bank.

European Central Bank (2004). *Convergence Report 2004.* Frankfurt am Main, Germany: European Central Bank.

European Central Bank (2006a). *Convergence Report May 2006.* Frankfurt am Main, Germany: European Central Bank.

European Central Bank (2006b). *Convergence Report December 2006.* Frankfurt am Main, Germany: European Central Bank.

European Central Bank (2007). *Convergence Report May 2007.* Frankfurt am Main, Germany: European Central Bank.

European Central Bank (2008a). *Convergence Report 2008.* Frankfurt am Main, Germany: European Central Bank.

European Central Bank (2008b). *Monthly Bulletin, 10th Anniversary of the ECB.* Frankfurt am Main, Germany: European Central Bank.

European Central Bank (2008c). *The European Central Bank, the Eurosystem, the European System of Central Banks,* 2nd Ed. Frankfurt am Main, Germany: European Central Bank.

European Commission (1980). Annual Economic Review 1980-81. Brussels, Belgium: European Commission.

European Commission (1990). *Economic and Monetary Union; the Economic Rationale and Design of the System.* Brussels, Belgium: European Commission.

European Commission (1995). *Green Paper on the Practical Arrangements for the Introduction of the Single Currency*. Brussels, Belgium: European Commission.

European Commission (2008). *Convergence Report 2008*. Brussels: European Commission.

European Communities, Monetary Committee (1974). Compendium of Community Monetary Texts. Brussels and Luxembourg, Luxembourg: European Communities.

European Communities, Monetary Committee (1986). Compendium of Community Monetary Texts. Brussels and Luxembourg, Luxembourg: European Communities.

European Monetary Institute (1995a). *The Changeover to the Single Currency*. Frankfurt am Main, Germany: European Monetary Institute.

European Monetary Institute (1995b). *Progress Towards Convergence, Report Prepared in Accordance with Article 7 of the EMI Statute*. Frankfurt am Main, Germany: European Monetary Institute.

European Monetary Institute (1996). *Progress Towards Convergence 1996*. Frankfurt am Main, Germany: European Monetary Institute.

European Monetary Institute (1997a). *The Single Monetary Policy in Stage Three: Specification of the Operational Framework*. Frankfurt am Main, Germany: European Monetary Institute.

European Monetary Institute (1997b). *The European Monetary Institute*. Frankfurt am Main, Germany: European Monetary Institute.

European Monetary Institute (1998). *Convergence Report–Report Required by Article 109j of the Treaty Establishing the European Community*. Frankfurt am Main, Germany: European Monetary Institute.

Fagan, G. and Henry, J. (1998). Long run money demand in the EU: Evidence for area-wide aggregates. *Empirical Economics*, 23, 483–506.

Faig, M. (1988). Characterization of the optimal tax on money when it functions as a medium of exchange. *Journal of Monetary Economics*, 22, 137–148.

Fase, M.M.G. and Winder, C.C.A. (1998). Wealth and the demand for money in the European union. *Empirical Economics*, 23, 507–524.

Feldstein, M. (1983). Domestic saving and international capital movements in the long run and the short run. *European Economic Review*, 21, 129–151.

Feldstein, M. and Bacchetta, P. (1991). National saving and international investment. In *National Saving and Economic Performance*, B.D. Bernheim and J.B. Shoven (eds), Chicago: University of Chicago Press.

Feldstein, M. and Horioka, C. (1980). Domestic saving and international capital flows. *Economic Journal*, 90, 314–329.

Fisher, I. (1907). *The Rate of Interest*, New York: Macmillan.

Fisher, R.A. (1932). *Statistical Methods for Research Workers*, 4th Ed. Edinburgh: Oliver & Boyd.

Frankel, J.A., Dooley, M. and Mathieson, D. (1986). International capital mobility in developing countries vs. industrialized countries: What do saving-investment correlations tell us? NBER Working Paper, No. 2043.

Frankel, J., Schmukler, S.L. and Servén, L. (2004). Global transmission of interest rates: Monetary independence and currency regime. *Journal of International Money and Finance*, 23, 701–733.

Galbraith, J.W. and Tkacz, G. (2000). Testing for asymmetry in the link between the yield spread and output in the G-7 countries. *Journal of International Money and Finance*, 19, 657–672.

Gerdesmeiser, D. and Roffia, B. (2003). Empirical estimates of reaction functions for the Euro area. European Central Bank Working Paper, No. 206.

Gerlach, S. and Schnabel, G. (2000). The Taylor rule and interest rates in the EMU area. *Economics Letters*, 67, 165–171.

Gerlach, S. and Smets, F. (1997). The term structure of Euro-rates: Some evidence in support of the expectations hypothesis. *Journal of International Money and Finance*, 16, 305–321.

Golub, S.S. (1990). International capital mobility: Net versus gross stocks and flows. *Journal of International Money and Finance*, 9, 424–439.

Hakkio, C.S. and Rush, M. (1991). Is the budget deficits "too large?" *Economic Inquiry*, 29, 429–445.

Hall, A. D., Anderson, H. M. and Granger, C. W. J. (1992). A cointegration analysis of treasury bill yields. *Review of Economics and Statistics*, 74, 116–126.

Hamilton, J.D. (1983). Oil and the macroeconomy since World War II. *Journal of Political Economy*, 91, 228–248.

Hamilton, J.D. and Flavin, M.A. (1986). On the limitations of government borrowing: A framework for empirical testing. *American Economic Review*, 76, 808–816.

Hamilton, J.D. and Kim, D.H. (2002). A re-examination of the predictability of economic activity using the yield spread. *Journal of Money, Credit and Banking*, 34, 340–360.

Hamori, N. and Hamori, S. (1999). Stability of the money demand function in Germany. *Applied Economics Letters*, 6, 329–332.

Hamori, S. (2007). International Capital Flows and the Frankel-Dooley-Mathieson Puzzle. *Economics Bulletin*, 15(19), 1–12.

Hamori, S. and Hamori, N. (2007). Sources of Real and Nominal Exchange Rate Movements for the Euro. *Economics Bulletin*, 6(32), 1–10.

Hamori, S. and Hamori, N. (2008a). Demand for money in the euro area. *Economic Systems*, 32, 274–284.

Hamori, S. and Hamori, N. (2008b). An empirical analysis of real exchange rate movements in the euro. Forthcoming in *Applied Economics*.

Hamori, S. and Hamori, N. (2009a). On the sustainability of budget deficits in the euro area. *Economics Bulletin*, 29(1), 56–66.

Hamori, S. and Hamori, N. (2009b). International term structure of interest rates in the Euro area. *Applied Economics Letters*, 16, 1113–1116.

Hansen, L.P. (1982). Large sample properties of generalized method of moments estimators. *Econometrica*, 50, 1029–1054.

Ho, T.W. (2002). A panel co-integration approach to the investment-saving correlation. *Empirical Economics*, 27, 91–100.

Hardouveli, G. (1994). The term structure spread and future changes in long and short rates in the G7 countries. *Journal of Monetary Economics*, 33, 255–283.

Harvey C.R. (1988). The real term structure and consumption growth. *Journal of Financial Economics*, 22, 305–333.

Harvey C.R. (1989). Forecasts of economic growth from the bond and stock markets. *Financial Analysts Journal*, September/October, 38–45.

Harvey, C.R. (1991). The term structure and world economic growth. *Journal of Fixed Income*, 1, 7–19.

Harvey C.R. (1993). Term structure forecasts economic growth. *Financial Analysts Journal*, May/June, 6–8.

Hasse, R.H. (1990). The European Central Bank: Perspectives for a Further Development of the European Monetary System. Gutersloh: Bertelsmann Foundation.

Haubrich, J.G. and Dombrosky, A.M. (1996). Predicting real growth using the yield curve. *Federal Reserve Bank of Cleveland Economic Review*, 32, 26–35.

Haug, A.A. (1991). Co-integration and government borrowing constraints: Evidence for the United States. *Journal of Business and Economic Statistics*, 9, 97–101.

Hayashi, F. (2000). *Econometrics*. Princeton and Oxford: Princeton University Press.

Hayo, B. (1999). Estimating a European demand for money. *Scottish Journal of Political Economy*, 46, 221–244.

Im, K.S., Pesaran, M.H. and Shin, Y. (2003). Testing for unit roots in heterogeneous panels. *Journal of Econometrics*, 115, 53–74.

Johansen, S. (1991). Estimation and hypothesis testing of co-integration vectors in Gaussian vector autoregressive models. *Econometrica*, 59, 1551–1580.

Johansen, S. and Juselius, K. (1990). Maximum likelihood estimation and inferences on co-integration with applications to the demand for money. *Oxford Bulletin of Economics and Statistics*, 52, 169–210.

Kenen, P.B. and Meade, E.E. (2003). EU accession and the euro: close together or far apart? Policy Brief. Washington D.C.: Institute for International Economics.

Kimbrough, K.P. (1986a). Inflation, employment, and welfare in the presence of transaction costs. *Journal of Money, Credit and Banking*, 18, 127–140.

Kimbrough, K.P. (1986b). The optimum quantity of money rule in the theory of public finance. *Journal of Monetary Economics*, 18, 277–284.

King, R. and Kurmann, A. (2002). Expectations and the term structure of interest rates: Evidence and implications. *Federal Reserve Bank of Richmond Economic Quarterly*, 88, 49–95.

Kristen, P.G. (2003). Interest rate reaction functions and the Taylor rule in the euro area. European Central Bank Working Paper, No. 258.

Kugler, P. (1997). Central bank policy reaction and expectations hypothesis of the term structure. *International Journal of Financial and Economics*, 2, 217–224.

Lastrapes, W.D. (1992). Sources of fluctuations in real and nominal exchange rates. *Review of Economics & Statistics*, 74, 530–539.

Levin, A., Lin, C.F. and Chu, C.S.J. (2002). Unit root tests in panel data: Asymptotic and finite-sample properties. *Journal of Econometrics*, 108, 1–24.

Maddala, G.S. and Wu, S. (1999). A comparative study of unit root tests with panel data and a new simple test. *Oxford Bulletin of Economics and Statistics*, 61, 631–652.

Masera, R. (1988). European currency: An Italian view. In *The European Monetary System*. Giavazzi, F., Micossi, S. and Miller, M. (eds.), Cambridge: Cambridge University Press.

McDonald, R. (1996). Panel unit root tests and real exchange rates. *Economics Letters*, 50, 7–11.

Mulhearn, C. and Vane, H.R. (2008). *The Euro Its Origins, Development and Prospects*. Cheltenham: Edward Elgar.

Murphy, R.G. (1984). Capital mobility and the relationship between saving and investment flows. *Journal of International Money and Finance*, 3, 327–342.

Newey, W.K. and West, K.D. (1987). A simple, positive semi-definite, heteroscedasticity and autocorrelation consistent covariance matrix. *Econometrica*, 55, 703–708.

Noyer, C. (2001). "Challenges ahead": The accession process. Foreign and Commonwealth Office, London, 12 November 2001. (http://www.ecb.int/press/key/date/2001/html/sp01112.en.hmtl).

Obstfeld, M. (1986). Capital mobility in the world economy: Theory and measurement. *Carnegie-Rochester Conference Series on Public Policy*, 24, 55–104.

Obstfeld, M. (1995). International capital mobility in the 1990's. In *Understanding Interdependence: The Macroeconomics of the Open Economy*, P.B. Kenen (ed.), Princeton: Princeton University Press.

Pedroni, P. (1999). Critical values for co-integration tests in heterogeneous panels with multiple regressors. *Oxford Bulletin of Economics and Statistics*, 61, 653–670.

Pedroni, P. (2001). Purchasing power parity tests in co-integrated panels. *Review of Economics and Statistics*, 83, 727–731.

Pesaran M.H. (2004). General diagnostic tests for cross section dependence in panels. Cambridge Working Papers in Economics No. 435, University of Cambridge, and CESifo Working Paper Series No. 1229.

Pesaran, M.H. (2007). A simple panel unit root test in the presence of cross-section dependence. *Journal of Applied Econometrics*, 22, 265–312.

Phillips, P.C.B. and Perron, P. (1988). Testing for a unit root in time series regression. *Biometrika*, 75, 335–346.

Plosser, C.I. and Rouwenhorst, K.G. (1994). International term structure and real economic growth. *Journal of Monetary Economics*, 33, 133–155.

Rogers, J.H. (1999). Monetary shocks and real exchange rates. *Journal of International Economics*, 49, 269–288.

Siklos, P.L. and Wohar, M.E. (1996). Co-integration and the term structure: A multicountry comparison. *International Review of Economics and Finance*, 5, 21–34.

Spencer, P. (1997). Monetary integration and currency substitution in the EMS: The case for a European monetary aggregate. *European Economic Review*, 41, 1403–1419.

Stock, J.H. and Watson, M.W. (1993). A simple estimator of co-integrating vectors in higher order integrated systems. *Econometrica*, 61, 783–820.

Stockman, A.C. (1987). The equilibrium approach to exchange rates. *Federal Reserve Bank of Richmond Economic Review*, 73, 12–30.

Svensson, L.E.O. (1997). Inflation forecast targeting: Implementing and monitoring inflation targets. *European Economic Review*, 41, 1111–1146.

Svensson, L.E.O. (2007). Inflation targeting (http://www.princeton.edu/svensson/papers/ PalgraveIT.pdf).

Taylor, J.B. (1993). Discretion versus policy rules in practice. *Carnegie Rochester Conference Series on Public Policy*, 39, 195–214.

Tesar, L.L. (1991). Saving, investment and international capital flows. *Journal of International Economics*, 31, 69–89.

Trehan, B. and Walsh, C.E. (1988). Common trends, the government budget constraint, and revenue smoothing. *Journal of Economic Dynamics and Control*, 12, 425–444.

The Nikkei (1997). Basic course: EMU: the road to the euro.

Tillman, P. (2006). Inflation regimes in the US term structure of interest rates. (http://www.iiw.uni-bonn.de/tillmann/termstructure_EdMod.pdf).

Wang, T. (2004). China: Sources of real exchange rate fluctuations. International Monetary Fund Working Paper No. 04/18.

Wesche K. (1997). The stability of European money demand: An investigation of M3H. *Open Economies Review*, 8, 371–391.

Wilcox, D.W. (1989). The sustainability of government deficits: Implications of present-value borrowing constraint. *Journal of Money, Credit and Banking*, 21, 291–306.

Zhang, H. (1993). Treasury yield curves and co-integration. *Applied Economics*, 25, 361–367.

Index

a no-Ponzi game, 92
accelerationist Phillips curve, 61
accession countries, 145, 159
aggregate data, 35, 57
aggregate-spending equation, 61
augmented Dickey–Fuller (ADF) test,
  35, 65, 76, 128

Balassa–Samuelson effect, 173, 180
bivariate VAR, 126, 130
budget sustainability, 91, 96

CD statistics, 78
CIPS test, 82
convergence criteria, 143
Convergence Reports, 20
Council of the European Union, 17,
  90, 166
cross-section dependence (*CD*) test, 78
cross-section dependence, 73, 78, 84
cross-sectionally augmented DF
  regression (CADF), 80
cross-sectionally augmented version of
  the IPS (CIPS) test, 81
currency board arrangement, 171, 172,
  174
currency crisis, 156
CUSUM of squares test, 107

Delors Report, 11
Deutsche Bundesbank, 10, 156
dynamic ordinary least squares method
  (DOLS), 38, 42, 43, 45, 66, 68, 69

ECOFIN council, 17
Economic and Financial Affairs
  (ECOFIN) Council, 13, 84, 89, 147
Economic and Financial Committee
  (EFC), 17
Economic and Monetary Committee
  (EMC), 90
Economic and Monetary Union
  (EMU), 1, 12, 24, 29, 87, 143
economic convergence criteria, 24, 87
effective exchange rate, 127
EMU opt-out clauses, 147, 148, 151
EONIA: Euro Overnight Index
  Average, 71
ESCB, 21
euro area, 143
euro, 1, 17, 87, 143
European Central Bank (ECB), 14, 21,
  31, 59, 71, 87, 144
European Coal and Steel Community
  (ECSC), 29
European Commission, 1, 17, 89, 144
European Council, 25, 91

197